INSIDE THE MINDS

Assisting Clients with Reinsurance Issues

Leading Lawyers on Navigating Regulatory Complexities from State-to-State and Keeping Abreast of Key Court Decisions

ASPATORE

For additional copies or customer service inquiries, please e-mail west.customer.service@thomson.com.

ISBN 978-0-314-29276-6

Mat #41686689

ASPATORE

Aspatore Books, a Thomson Reuters business, exclusively publishes C-Level executives and partners from the world's most respected companies and law firms. Each publication provides professionals of all levels with proven business and legal intelligence from industry insiders—direct and unfiltered insight from those who know it best. Aspatore Books is committed to publishing an innovative line of business and legal titles that lay forth principles and offer insights that can have a direct financial impact on the reader's business objectives.

Each chapter in the *Inside the Minds* series offers thought leadership and expert analysis on an industry, profession, or topic, providing a future-oriented perspective and proven strategies for success. Each author has been selected based on their experience and C-Level standing within the business and legal communities. *Inside the Minds* was conceived to give a first-hand look into the leading minds of top business executives and lawyers worldwide, presenting an unprecedented collection of views on various industries and professions.

Praise for *Inside the Minds*

"This series provides a practical and focused discussion of the leading issues in law today." – John V. Biernacki, Partner, Jones Day

"*Inside the Minds* draws from the collective experience of the best professionals. The books are informative from an academic, and, more importantly, practical perspective. I highly recommend them." – Keith M. Aurzada, Partner, Bryan Cave LLP

"Aspatore's *Inside the Minds* series provides practical, cutting edge advice from those with insight into the real world challenges that confront businesses in the global economy." – Michael Bednarek, Partner, Shearman & Sterling LLP

"What to read when you want to be in the know—topical, current, practical, and useful information on areas of the law that everyone is talking about." – Erika L. Morabito, Partner, Patton Boggs LLP

"Some of the best insight around from sources in the know" – Donald R. Kirk, Shareholder, Fowler White Boggs PA

"The *Inside the Minds* series provides a unique window into the strategic thinking of key players in business and law." – John M. Sylvester, Partner, K&L Gates LLP

"Comprehensive analysis and strategies you won't find anywhere else." – Stephen C. Stapleton, Of Counsel, Dykema Gossett PLLC

"The *Inside the Minds* series is a real hands-on, practical resource for cutting edge issues." – Trey Monsour, Partner, Haynes and Boone LLP

"A tremendous resource, amalgamating commentary from leading professionals that is presented in a concise, easy to read format." – Alan H. Aronson, Shareholder, Akerman Senterfitt

"Unique and invaluable opportunity to gain insight into the minds of experienced professionals." – Jura C. Zibas, Partner, Lewis Brisbois Bisgaard & Smith LLP

"A refreshing collection of strategic insights, not dreary commonplaces, from some of the best of the profession." – Roger J. Magnuson, Partner, Dorsey & Whitney LLP

"Provides valuable insights by experienced practitioners into practical and theoretical developments in today's ever-changing legal world." – Elizabeth Gray, Partner, Willkie, Farr & Gallagher LLP

"This series provides invaluable insight into the practical experiences of lawyers in the trenches." – Thomas H. Christopher, Partner, Kilpatrick Stockton LLP

Contents

Making Informed Decisions When Preparing for the Future of Reinsurance Regulation

David W. Deal

JD, MBA, CPCU, CCP, ARe, ASLI, ARC

Senior Counsel, Insurance Industry Team

Holland & Knight LLP

ASPATORE

Introduction

Reinsurance transactions are often poorly understood by attorneys who do not spend a substantial amount of time focusing in this specific area. For the uninformed, the focus seems to be limited to claim handling issues and underwriting issues, but frequently ignores critical regulatory issues.

Reinsurance transactions tend to be very large exposure transactions with significant reliance on actuarial estimates and business projects, which can end up being significantly wrong in the future. When these transactions prove unprofitable or are challenged by regulators, attorneys who advised on or drafted the transaction can be faced with large and complex malpractice allegations. There are only two intelligent ways for an attorney to avoid these downstream backlashes: either seek the assistance of another attorney with significant experience in the area, or spend the time becoming deeply and broadly educated in the area of reinsurance. This discussion attempts to provide you with a head start on the latter by explaining foundational concepts, providing a historical context for reinsurance regulation, outlining the current regulatory structure, and giving you a glimpse into possible future changes in those structures.

The Importance of Understanding Reinsurance Regulation

Attorneys often fail to appreciate the importance of understanding reinsurance as a distinct area of law, especially reinsurance regulation. Such understanding is essential for several reasons. First, it obviously prevents regulatory violations. Companies do not want to damage their reputations in the industry; nor do they want to fall out of the regulators' good graces.

Second, from a business perspective, to participate in the market effectively, compliance with certain direct and indirect regulations is essential, because, in most instances, ceding insurers have no interest in a reinsurer if the ceding company cannot obtain credit for the reinsurance on their balance sheet.

Third, the reinsurance contract can end up being treated as conforming to the regulations, even if it is not written with this intent. This means clients may end up with a contract they did not expect, which can further present exposures they did not properly account for in the pricing and other components of the contract consideration.

Fourth, reinsurance regulation affects related rules of law. For example, while there may not be many regulations specifically governing reinsurance of claims or underwriting issues, case law and other related industry practices are abundant, and in significant ways they relate to the fundamental concept of how reinsurance is regulated and its purpose. Understanding the reinsurance regulation framework informs an attorney's ability to understand and advise on issues driven by related rules of law, even in areas that are not specifically regulated.

Foundational Concepts of Reinsurance

Attorneys need to understand some foundational concepts in reinsurance before they can begin to understand reinsurance regulation or anything else in this arena. The technical definition of a reinsurance agreement is a contract in which one insurer agrees to indemnify another insurer against loss or liability, the risk of which the latter has assumed under a separate and distinct contract as an insurer of a third party. A less artful way I often hear this described is that reinsurance is insurance for an insurance company, which can be misleading. Although both insurance and reinsurance provide risk transfer, they are different in terms of parties, purposes, and performance. These distinctions mean that some of the principles applicable to interpretation and enforcement of an insurance policy are not applicable to a reinsurance contract.

To appreciate these distinctions, the foundational structure of reinsurance needs to be understood. To start, at the most fundamental level, an insurer can transfer risk through either facultative or treaty reinsurance. From these two building blocks come a host of hybrid forms of reinsurance, which fulfill unique needs in the market.

Facultative Reinsurance

Facultative reinsurance is the reinsurance of risk on a single policy issued by the reinsured insurance company, often called the "direct insurer." Facultative reinsurance is underwritten for each cession by which the direct insurer cedes all or part of its risk to the reinsurer. The reinsurer can approve or deny each individual risk, and can tailor the price for each risk. This risk-by-risk decision can be on an excess basis, meaning the reinsurer is liable for the loss in excess of a stated amount, or on a pro rata basis, meaning the reinsurer is liable for a proportional amount of loss attributable to the underwritten risk. The proportional amount of the loss can either be by quota share, where the reinsurer is liable for a percentage of all the loss, or by surplus share, where the reinsurer is liable for a percentage of the loss in excess of a certain amount.

A facultative contract does not generally contemplate a reinsurer administering and handling the reinsured's claims and other practices. Rather, the insurer retains those duties. Because of this, the insurer is expected to retain enough risk to give the reinsurer comfort that the policy will be well administered.

Treaty Reinsurance

Treaty reinsurance is a contract for a period of time to reinsure multiple risks. The contract is essentially an agreement by the reinsurer to pick up all risks falling within a certain category of policies that have been or will be written by the insurer. It can begin with the reinsurer being obligated to do nothing but wait for the insured to write a risk, or it can start at the outset by ceding existing policies. Treaty reinsurance usually insures losses directly underwritten during the agreed term or losses occurring during the term on policies written prior to the term. The scope of the reinsurance is usually defined as a certain class of policies, a certain type of business, or an entire book. The premiums can be structured in various ways, but they are typically either based directly on the premiums of the underlying policy, or are a lump or variable sum based on the expected losses and/or premiums for the underlying business.

Treaty reinsurance frequently is used for surplus relief for the ceding insurer. Subject to certain requirements discussed later, a ceding insurer can take credit for the reinsurance on its balance sheet. As a matter of mechanics, when an insurer writes an insurance policy, a liability for the unearned premium is accounted for on its balance sheet. A treaty reinsurance agreement allows the ceding company to transfer to the reinsurer a portion of the unearned premium liability. Also, the treaty includes a ceding commission paid by the reinsurer to the insurer, which adds to the surplus of the insurer. These two effects keep the insurer's capital-to-premium ratio higher than it would be if there was no reinsurance, enabling the insurer to continue writing business it may otherwise have had insufficient capital to write. Of course, treaty reinsurance also has other benefits for the insurer, for example, helping the insurer diversify its risk.

Other Forms and Uses of Reinsurance

There are also more novel forms and uses of reinsurance. For example, in a typical fronting arrangement, a reinsurer that is not licensed to write certain business has a licensed insurance company write it and send all the risk up to the reinsurer. In a pooling agreement, risks are pooled from amongst a group of companies and redistributed between the group. This allows the companies to share the risk among themselves, which diversifies the risk across the group. Captive reinsurance allows an insurer to move its risk to another entity for various purposes (for example, tax relief). In portfolio reinsurance, the reinsurer assumes an entire book of business, usually because the insurer is withdrawing from a business or liquidating the company. This is similar to the run-off contracts used at Lloyd's of London, where the names of the syndicate change periodically and there is a need to end the contract with one list of names and pass on the exposure to the new list. Catastrophe bonds are frequently thought of as reinsurance because the insurer typically purchases reinsurance from a special-purpose vehicle established to facilitate the issuance of bonds to investors, which are essentially an advance of money at a higher rate than usual, to be repaid to the extent it is not consumed by specific losses. In financial (or finite) reinsurance, an insurance company receives a sum of money from the reinsurer and pays a premium for it in the future. In all types of reinsurance, pro rata and excess mechanisms can be combined in almost limitless ways based on the amount of participation, whether there are variable attachment points,[1] and the methods of calculating the premium.

---

[1] "Attachment points" are the dollar value where the reinsured's risk ends and the reinsurer's risk begins. This is conceptually similar to a deductible or self-insured retention that might be in a primary policy.

Relationships Often Confused with Reinsurance

People tend to confuse certain relationships with reinsurance; take, for example, a novation. When a portfolio transfer occurs, the ceding company reinsures a full portfolio. The insurance company is still in direct privity with the insured, but all of the risk is reinsured. As a result, the reinsurer has no direct financial exposure to the original insured (at least, in theory). This is a reinsurance relationship. In contrast, a novation takes the portfolio concept one step further and actually *replaces* the insurer with the reinsurer. This scenario cannot technically be reinsurance because the original direct insurer has been removed from the equation. Instead, the reinsurer is now the direct insurer.

Self-insurance is also sometimes confused with reinsurance. If the reinsurer retains control over direct insurance liabilities it has made, such as its employee benefits liabilities, this arrangement is self-insurance not reinsurance. Similarly, double insurance (when multiple policies cover the same interest) is not reinsurance. Excess insurance is not reinsurance because there is no direct relationship between the reinsurer and the insured, and co-insurance is not reinsurance because all of the insurers have a direct relationship with the insured.

Some people also think indemnification agreements, such as service contracts or even standalone agreements, are reinsurance. They are not. The obligee is not an insurer, so the transaction cannot be reinsurance. Partnerships and joint ventures are not reinsurance.

Banking relationships are not reinsurance. There is no deposit put on hold with a reinsurer because a deposit means the insurer is guaranteed to get the deposited amount back at the end of the relationship with interest and, therefore, there is no transfer of risk. Any time there is a guaranteed return or a guarantee of no loss, risk has not been transferred, and the relationship is not an insurance relationship.

It is important to understand what types of relationships constitute reinsurance. At times people either apply reinsurance concepts to contracts that are not reinsurance, or fail to apply reinsurance regulations to relationships that are, in fact, reinsurance. Doing this results in a host of problems such as wrongly applying regulatory constraints to a non-reinsurance agreement, violating regulations by not following applicable regulatory rules for a reinsurance agreement, accounting discrepancies, miscalculation of risks and benefits under the contract, or incorrect application of related concepts.

Reinsurance Regulation: A Brief History

Reinsurance has been around for hundreds of years, but its regulation has largely developed in the latter part of the twentieth century. The most recent shift in reinsurance policy has resulted from the enactment of the Dodd–Frank Wall Street Reform and Consumer Protection Act (the Dodd-Frank Act).[2] The Dodd-Frank Act, as well as the state and federal reverberations in its wake, give us some indication of what is likely to happen in the future in the area of reinsurance regulation.

Settling into a State-Based Insurance Regulatory System (1945–1982)

Prior to 1944, insurance was regulated at the state level. In 1944, however, the Supreme Court held, in a case called *United States v. South-Eastern Underwriters Association*,[3] that federal antitrust laws applied to insurance, which called into serious question whether state regulations (e.g., those governing joint underwriting and joint rate setting) were preempted. In an unusual move, the next year the federal government decided it did not want to regulate insurance, and passed the McCarran-Ferguson Act of 1945,[4] which basically reversed the *South-eastern Underwriters*[5] decision. It dictated that silence on the part of Congress was not a barrier to regulation or taxation of the "business of insurance" by the states. Thus, states were expressly free to regulate the "business of insurance" unless Congress enacted laws that (i) specifically addressed the "business of insurance" and (ii) were explicitly preemptive of, or contrary to, state insurance regulations. The McCarran-Ferguson Act also provided that insurers could engage in joint underwriting and joint rate setting as long as those activities were regulated by states and as long as insurers and producers did not engage in

---

[2] Dodd-Frank Act, Pub. L. No. 111–203, 124 Stat. 1376-2223 (2010).
[3] *United States v. S.E. Underwriters Ass'n*, 322 U.S. 533 (1944).
[4] McCarran-Ferguson Act of 1945, 15 U.S.C. §§ 1011-1015 .
[5] *S.E. Underwriters Ass'n*, 322 U.S. 533.

boycotts, coercion, or intimidation. The regulatory structure that built on that foundation during the next forty years created our present-day relationship between insurer and regulator. It set the parameters regarding the type of policy that could be issued, and the policy's reliability, interpretation, and enforcement.

The great debate over those decades has been what constitutes the "business of insurance." Some states followed the three-part analysis to determine whether an activity constituted the "business of insurance": (1) whether the activity involved spreading the policy owner's risk, (2) whether the activity was an integral part of the relationship of the insurer and the insured, and (3) whether the activity was limited to entities within the insurance industry. If the activity passed that test, it was considered the "business of insurance" and was regulated by the states. As fallout from the enactment of the McCarran-Ferguson Act, the National Association of Insurance Commissioners (NAIC), which is made up of the insurance commissioners of each state, created model laws for individual states to enact to occupy this regulatory field and thereby retain the preemption afforded to them by the McCarren-Ferguson Act. By the early 1980s, a well-developed insurance regulatory structure existed across the states. While these general rules affected reinsurance to the extent that any general insurance rule applied to reinsurance (see below), reinsurance as a target of specific regulation seemed to remain under the regulators' radar.

Reinsurance Gains Regulatory Attention (1982–Present)

Many reinsurers went bankrupt in the 1970s, and reinsurance was officially on the regulators' radar. In 1982, the NAIC formed an advisory committee on reinsurance for the first time. A couple of years later, it approved NAIC Credit for Reinsurance Model Law. Between that time and 2008, the reinsurance area did not change again dramatically. In 2008, however, the federal government began looking once again at what to do with regard to insurance companies during the financial crisis. The NAIC tried to preempt an expansion of federal control into the area that had become comfortably occupied by state regulation over the prior decades. The NAIC's effort on this front specific to reinsurance was to create the Reinsurance Regulatory

Modernization Framework[6] proposal. The framework was designed to apply a rating-based sliding scale to determine collateral requirements for non-admitted reinsurers, rather than requiring the 100 percent collateralization that was currently used in the states. Ultimately, the proposal could not get Congressional support, but it was revived, in spirit, in the Dodd-Frank Act[7] as a subchapter entitled the "Nonadmitted and Reinsurance Reform Act of 2010 (NRRA)."[8] The Dodd-Frank Act[9] was passed on July 21, 2010, although most of it did not become effective until July 21, 2011.

Under the NRRA,[10] non-domiciliary states are prohibited from denying credit for reinsurance if the domiciliary state of the ceding insurer recognizes the credit. This was an attempt to resolve the lack of uniformity amongst the states that the federal government seemed to blame for the financial crisis, while not actually changing the state-based regulatory system.

The Modern Reinsurance Regulation Rubric

Reinsurers can cross the threshold into a jurisdiction for purposes of regulation in three ways. First, the reinsurer can be domiciled in the jurisdiction, which established the general jurisdiction of the local regulators. Second, a reinsurer domiciled outside the jurisdiction can obtain authorization to transact insurance in the local jurisdiction, in which case the reinsurer essentially concedes to the oversight of the local regulators. Third, a reinsurance contract can call for application of local regulatory law, although such contracts are atypical. For purposes of the below discussion, the assumption is that the reinsurer has undertaken one of these actions, which establish the fundamental jurisdictional authority of the local regulators. Without these, reinsurers are largely unregulated locally.

---

[6] *See* NAIC Memo: Reinsurance (E) Committee Task Force Activities (Sept. 12, 2008).
[7] Dodd–Frank Act.
[8] Nonadmitted and Reinsurance Reform Act. Pub. L. No. 111-203, §§ 511-542, 124 Stat. 1589 (2010) (codified at 15 U.S.C. §§ 8201-8232).
[9] Dodd–Frank Act.
[10] Nonadmitted and Reinsurance Reform Act.

Assuming the foundational jurisdiction discussed above is established, reinsurers are governed by three different types of regulations, the amalgamation of which results in the reinsurance regulation rubric: general regulations governing insurers generally and which are directly applicable to reinsurers, regulations specifically applicable to reinsurers, and regulations governing insurers that indirectly impact reinsurers.

Regulations Governing Insurers Generally

Many states consider a reinsurer merely a type of insurer and, therefore, generally require reinsurers to comply with all of the state laws any ordinary insurance company must comply with. Some states (including Illinois) even use the term "reinsurer" as a subset of the "insurer" definition. Other states have a separate category of entity for reinsurers. Regardless of this distinction, as a practical matter, most states regulate reinsurers in many ways the same as insurers, while providing exemptions from certain rules. For this reason, counsel must be familiar with the rules in the applicable states to determine if and how they specifically apply to a reinsurer. When determining which direct insurance regulations apply to a reinsurer, the attorney needs to ask multiple questions. Does the state's specific definition of the term "insurer" include a reinsurer? Does the specific rule define its own scope in such a way as to expressly or implicitly include reinsurers? How does the state generally treat reinsurance under other rules? Does the activity being regulated pass the aforementioned three-part test to qualify as the "business of insurance"? If not, it may be preempted by federal law. This analysis will result in many general insurance rules being applied to reinsurers.

In addition to regulations that apply to insurers, there are general business regulations that apply broadly to all corporations doing business, which frequently include insurance companies. This set of general state and federal rules generally applies to reinsurers to the same extent as they do to any other entity deemed to be doing business within any particular jurisdiction.

At the end of the day, the list of direct general regulations that typically apply to reinsurers runs a wide gamut, including the following examples:

- Reinsurers must comply with their corporate charters
- Reinsurers are subject to tax laws at the federal and state levels
- Reinsurers are authorized to cede risks to an assuming entity
- Foreign insurers must deposit money or file a bond in the local jurisdiction to ensure payment of any judgment before they can file a responsive pleading
- Reinsurers are exempt from federal bankruptcy laws
- Reinsurers must screen their officers and directors for fitness
- Reinsurers have limits on their investments
- Reinsurers must allow the Department of Insurance to conduct periodic evaluations of assets and statutory reserving requirements
- Reinsurers are restricted in their ability to claim credit for reinsurance purchased
- Reinsurers are subject to state Unfair Insurance Practices Acts[11]
- Reinsurers are subject to state Unfair Claims Settlement Practices Acts[12]
- Reinsurers are within the purview of the Federal Arbitration Act[13]

If the reinsurer does nothing to establish the jurisdiction of local regulators (e.g., obtaining a certificate of authority or establishing a local domicile), the reinsurer is largely unaffected by the above rules. In the event that the reinsurance agreement calls for the application of local state law, however, plaintiffs have argued that some of the above rules could be deemed applicable to certain reinsurance claims or transactions, such as a local Unfair Insurance Practices Act or Unfair Claims Settlement Practices Act. While these rules are neither "regulation" in the strictest sense, nor arguably intended or designed to apply to reinsurers, many reinsurers opt to either apply the law of their domicile to the contract or do not designate a specific state's law under the choice of law provision. Because most reinsurance contracts call for arbitration, which necessarily applies the customs and

[11] *See, e.g.*, Cal. Ins. Code § 790; Ga. Code Ann., § 33-6-5; Mass. Gen. Laws ch. 93A § 9; N.M. Stat. Ann. § 59A-16-1 (1978).

[12] Insurance consumer protection statutes are known by various names, such as: "Unfair Insurance Practices," "Unfair Settlement Practices," "Unfair Claims Settlement Practices." Steven Pitt et al., Couch on Ins. 1 § 4:20 (3d ed. 1995).

[13] Federal Arbitration Act, Pub. L. No. 68–401, 43 Stat. 883(1925) (codified at 9 U.S.C. §§ 1-16).

practices of the industry over technical rules of law, the omission of a state's choice of law rules can be a beneficial way to avoid unintentionally applying a local statutory scheme to the reinsurance agreement. The drawback is that some disputes turn on whether a certain local "flavor" of a set of rules is applicable, such as nuances regarding "follow the fortunes" and other claim payment principles. If no state is chosen, the arbitrators have the power to determine which "flavor" of the rule the parties intended to apply to the transaction.

Reinsurance-Specific Regulations

Some rules are written specifically for reinsurers. For example, some states specifically authorize or deny authority to write reinsurance. States often restrict mutual companies from writing reinsurance. Reinsurance intermediaries' licensing, duties, and contract provisions are regulated. Additionally, some states regulate the cession of particular types of insurance, such as the reinsurance of title exposures, mutual company exposures, or reciprocal reinsurance. Some states authorize certain specific reinsurers, such as Lloyd's of London, or permit the reinsurance of specific types of risks, such as those related to worker's compensation, health maintenance organizations, property and casualty, or fraternal benefits societies. Some types of reinsurance are region-specific, such as mine subsidence, hail, and tornado reinsurance. Other states have created rules regarding the combination of reinsurers or reinsurance pooling, as well as special rules directed at foreign reinsurers.

Indirect Regulations

One of the most important "regulations" governing reinsurance is actually not a regulation of reinsurers at all, but instead a regulation of insurers that so heavily impacts reinsurers that reinsurers must address the issue constantly. The rules governing an insurer's ability to take balance sheet credit related to reinsurance it purchases is fundamental to most reinsurance purchasing decisions. To be clear, the regulations governing reinsurers do not require them to be admitted in a state to write a reinsurance contract covering risks in that state; however, if the insurance company conducts business with a reinsurer that is not an authorized insurer, the insurer is not permitted to take any credit for the reinsurance on its balance sheet, which results in the insurer not receiving any surplus relief, which is usually a key business driver for the purchase of the reinsurance. For the insurer to obtain balance sheet credit, the reinsurer must either be authorized (in which case it will be regulated as an authorized insurer), or it must post collateral in the form of a trust, letter of credit, or funds-withheld account.

Each of these forms of collateral has its benefits and drawbacks, and depending on the exact factors at play in a deal, any one of them may be more favorable to the specific deal. A funds-withheld account is very easy to manage compared to a trust. However, the funds-withheld account remains within the control of the insurer, which is generally unacceptable to the reinsurer. A trust carries some administrative costs and operational processes to manage, but it is usually more palatable to the reinsurer. A letter of credit is relatively simple to purchase and maintain but generally incurs a high carrying cost.

Regardless of what method the parties use to collateralize the unauthorized reinsurance, the reinsurer must also submit to the jurisdiction of any court in that state or authorize an attorney to accept service of process, and the reinsurer must assume full payment of the reinsured's obligations without regard to payments made under the underlying policies in the event of the underlying solvency. Some states have even prohibited reinsurers from offsetting money owed to the reinsurer under the reinsurance agreement by money owed to it by an insolvent reinsured to maximize the bankruptcy estate of an insured. In this manner, by regulating insurers' credit for reinsurance, the regulators are able to indirectly regulate even reinsurers which do not have a local certificate of authority.

The Impact of the Dodd-Frank Act[14] on the Existing Reinsurance Regulatory Framework

In 2010, we saw Congress trying to untangle serious issues in the financial industry. For the most part, insurance companies were not held responsible for the financial crisis. Those insurers who did play a role, such as AIG, played a role largely with their *non-insurance* practices. Congress ultimately

[14] Dodd–Frank Act.

rolled out 800 pages of legislation—the Dodd-Frank Act[15]—aimed at fixing the issues it identified as causing problems in the financial system. Out of those 800 pages, only twenty are dedicated to insurance (the NRRA). Most of the NRRA addresses the need for uniformity amongst the various state rules governing surplus lines and reinsurance.

The Dodd-Frank Act[16] created the Federal Insurance Office (FIO), which is based in the Treasury Department. Although not vested with specific regulatory powers, the FIO covers all lines of insurance except for health insurance policies, stand-alone long-term care policies, and crop insurance. It monitors and reports on the insurance industry, coordinates insurance issues, and recommends to the Financial Stability Oversight Council (FSOC) which organizations should be included on its list of the "systemically important financial institutions." The FSOC was set up to govern entities that are deemed "too big to fail" because their failure will have a systemic impact on the economy. Being on the systemically risky list means the insurer is not only regulated by any relevant states in which it operates, but also regulated at the federal level by the Federal Reserve Board. So far the FSOC has designated AIG and Prudential as "systemically important" and is considering adding MetLife to that list.

The Dodd-Frank Act[17] also created a "home state" concept intended to resolve the lack of uniformity among the states on various issues. This was important because in each interstate transaction, regulators from every affected state frequently claimed they had the right to regulate the insurer or reinsurer in some form. It was not unusual to have conflicting or additive rules, leaving an insurer or reinsurer who wanted to comply confused about how to do so or burdened by the compliance requirements.

As it pertains to reinsurance, Section 531 of the Dodd-Frank Act[18] dictates that the application of credit for reinsurance rules be based solely on the domiciliary state of the reinsurer, and that only the domiciliary state of the ceding company may regulate the transaction.

---

15 *Id.*
16 *Id.*
17 *Id.*
18 *Id.*

The intended result is that multiple sets of rules can no longer compete for application. It also preempted certain state insurance laws to the extent they were inconsistent with bilateral or multilateral agreements entered into with the United States and foreign nations. This essentially forces state regulators to comply with federal treaties. It also preempted state insurance laws that were discriminatory toward non-US insurers. The act explicitly deems certain types of laws to be within the sole purview of the states, including rules regarding insurers' rates, premiums, underwriting, and sales practices.

What Does the Future Hold for Reinsurance Regulation?

The FIO's job is to evaluate the insurance industry, determine what does not work, and make recommendations for changes to keep the industry healthy. The office released its first report, *How to Modernize and Improve the System of Insurance Regulation in the United States* (the *Modernization Report*),[19] on December 12, 2013. While its recommendations do not have the force of law, they serve as an indicator to the NAIC and state insurance departments of what the federal regulators believe should be the priorities and policies at the state level. If the state commissioners are not responsive to these issues, a future Dodd-Frank Act[20] could establish federal rules to address the issues the federal regulators believe were not adequately addressed by the state regulators. With this in mind, states will probably attempt to respond to the recommendations in the report and show the federal government they have put in place mitigations and solutions for the risks the FIO has identified.

The *Modernization Report* found that insurers and state regulators are not adequately meeting the needs of a global industry. As a result, the FIO recommends federal government involvement to help bring uniformity, efficiency, and consistency to the industry. However, the FIO does not recommend the federal government take over regulation of the insurance industry. Instead, the FIO recommends the creation of a complementary structure dovetailing the efforts of federal and state regulators to build uniformity and ease its inefficiencies and burdens.

---

[19] US Dep't of the Treasury, *How to Modernize and Improve the System of Insurance Regulation in the United States* (2013).
[20] Dodd–Frank Act.

The FIO suggested that the focus of regulators' efforts should be on modernizing state-by-state regulation. Many of the individual recommendations are not directly relevant to reinsurers unless they are also subject to regulation as an admitted or domiciled insurer. The items relevant to reinsurers specifically are listed below:

- Develop a uniform oversight regime for the transfer of risk for reinsurance captives
- Monitor the impact of different regulation regimes on different markets to determine the best practices for fostering competitive markets
- Identify best practices to mitigate losses from natural catastrophes

In the *Modernization Report*, the FIO also advocated specific areas of federal involvement:

- Mortgage-related issues
- A national reinsurance collateral requirements rule based on the NAIC Credit for Reinsurance Model Law and Regulation[21]
- Supervisory colleges to monitor financial stability in large nationally and internationally active insurers

Conclusion

To effectively counsel clients in matters related to reinsurance, attorneys need to have a strong understanding of what reinsurance is, what it is intended to do, how it is structured, how it is regulated today, and how it may be regulated in the future. Without this understanding, attorneys put their clients at risk (and their own malpractice policies). With this understanding, attorneys have a valuable understanding of how claims will arise, how underwriting issues may develop, how reinsurance contracts could be treated in a liquidation, how insurers may (or may not) account for the reinsurance under statutory accounting rules, and a myriad of other critical legal data points.

---

[21] *See* NAIC, Credit for Reinsurance Model Insurance Law (2012), *available at* www.naic.org/store/free/MDL-785.pdf; *see also* NAIC, Credit for Reinsurance Model Insurance Regulation (2012), *available at www.naic.org/store/free/MDL-786.pdf.*

Key Takeaways

- Gain a thorough understanding of reinsurance regulation to prevent your clients from committing regulatory violations, thereby protecting their reputations in the industry, keeping them in the regulators' good graces, and allowing them to participate effectively in the marketplace.
- Understand what types of relationships constitute reinsurance. Avoid unnecessarily hampering non-reinsurance transactions with reinsurance compliance obligations or failing to apply mandatory regulations to reinsurance transactions.
- Become familiar with the rules in applicable states to determine if and how they specifically apply to a reinsurer. Understand the preemptive effect of Section 531 of the Dodd-Frank Act on state reinsurance regulations. Determine if the relevant states exempt reinsurers from the rule at issue or create additional requirements.
- Be prepared for the modernization of state-by-state insurance regulation, as well as continued federal involvement in certain areas intended to build uniformity and ease the inefficiencies and burdens caused by the lack thereof.

David W. Deal, JD, MBA, CPCU, CCP, ARe, ASLI, ARC, is senior counsel of Holland & Knight LLP's Insurance Industry Team in the firm's San Francisco office. His practice focuses on counseling companies on strategic legal issues, advising on regulatory matters, and designing corporate transactions. His clients have included the boards of directors, executive management, and shareholders of admitted and surplus lines insurance companies and reinsurers, agents and brokers, and other intermediaries.

Prior to joining Holland & Knight LLP, Mr. Deal served as the general counsel of the GeoVera Group (formerly USF&G). He has also been a senior lawyer in the General Counsel's Office of Fireman's Fund Insurance Company (Allianz of America), as well as a private practice attorney counseling banks and insurance entities.

Dealing with Key Issues in Reinsurance Litigation or Arbitration

Barry R. Ostrager

Partner

Simpson Thacher & Bartlett LLP

ASPATORE

Introduction

This chapter discusses the fundamentals of reinsurance. The author is the co-author of two authoritative treatises on insurance and reinsurance law: *The Handbook on Insurance Coverage Disputes* (Aspen 2013, Sixteenth Edition) and *Modern Reinsurance Law and Practice* (Thomson Reuters 2014, Third Edition).[1] This chapter explains the role reinsurance plays in the transfer of risks in the insurance industry.

Understanding Reinsurance

Reinsurance is a mechanism for spreading risk. There is a long history of reinsurance serving as an effective risk transfer mechanism. So, an individual or corporation that is exposed to risk purchases *direct* insurance from a property insurer, a comprehensive general liability insurer, or a directors and officers insurer; those direct insurers—which also have a pool of risks—cede by treaty or by facultative certificate those risks to reinsurers. Those reinsurers, in turn, further allocate their risk by dealing with retrocessionaires, which are insurers of reinsurers. Those retrocessionaires typically further retrocede the risks. In other words, a large group of individual risks get spread out through the international insurance markets so that in the event of a catastrophic loss, no one individual and no one company sustains the entire loss.

While the basic reinsurance practices/mechanisms I have described have not greatly changed in the past five years, there are now some new players that participate in the reinsurance markets, and there are some reinsurers that have greater appetites for risk and consequently do not retrocede portions of risks. There are also reinsurers that purchase run-off obligations of direct insurers (such as Berkshire Hathaway), as well as direct insurers that have a greater appetite for risk and therefore retain larger portions of risks they might have historically reinsured.

Facultative reinsurance is typically utilized for a single unique risk as opposed to a pool of risks. For example, if a property insurer decided to

[1] Barry R. Ostrager & Thomas R. Newman, *Handbook on Insurance Coverage Disputes* (16th ed. 2012); Barry Ostrager & Mary Vyskocil, *Modern Reinsurance Law and Practice* (3d ed. 2014).

insure just one property (e.g., the World Trade Center), that insurer might enter into a facultative reinsurance contract to deal with that specific risk. Treaty reinsurance is, as the name suggests, an agreement that covers a particular product line of insurance or a particular geographic area. For example, an insurer might have treaty reinsurance for all of the business a direct insurer does with respect to automobile insurance in the state of New York.

It should be noted that there are reinsurers that are qualified to do business in the United States, and there are reinsurers that are not qualified to do business in the United States but are nevertheless available marketplaces to direct insurers and reinsurers. Whatever form of coverage that is written can be reinsured. Again, comprehensive general liability, directors and officers, and errors and omissions insurers are trying to transfer risk in such a way that no individual participant absorbs an unacceptable degree of loss.

The basic concept of insurance is that an insurer that insures 200,000 homes is going to pay for property damage that occurs in some subset of those 200,000 homes, but it is exceedingly unlikely that the insurer is going to have to pay claims on all 200,000 homes. In other words, by virtue of writing a large volume of insurance, the insurer is spreading its risk, and by securing treaty reinsurance the insurer is further spreading risk. Again, it is common for virtually all direct insurers of all lines of business to purchase reinsurance; depending on a particular company's appetite for risk, an insurer may cede as much as 100 percent of the risk to reinsurers, or as little as 20 percent.

Recent Laws and Decisions Impacting the Area of Reinsurance Law

The most important principle of reinsurance law is the Follow the Fortunes Doctrine,[2] which holds that when a direct insurer pays a claim in good faith, the reinsurer has to follow the direct insurer's fortunes—i.e., accept the claim payment or settlement as reasonable. This is an issue that is frequently litigated in a variety of contexts.

[2] John T. Harding, *The English Revolution: "Follow the Fortunes" After Lexington v. Agf and Wasa*, 77 Def. Couns. J. 328, 332 (2010).

There is a recent New York Court of Appeals decision in the *McArthur* [3] case that further clarifies the doctrine in New York. I believe this decision fundamentally reaffirms the vitality of the Follow the Fortunes Doctrine, with minor some clarifications.

Insurance law is entirely a creature of state law; therefore, whatever state law is applicable to an insurance contract controls the disposition of cases involving that insurance contract. Most reinsurance treaties and facultative certificates, but not all, provide for resolution of disputes by arbitration, and those arbitrations may be seated in New York, London, Bermuda, Hong Kong, or elsewhere. Also, certain treaties may or may not specify a particular law as being applicable to any dispute that arises out of the reinsurance relationship. When courts deal with insurance and reinsurance law issues, they follow well-established principles that have been actively litigated for decades. There is a very well-developed body of law relating to the rights and obligations of insureds, insurers, and reinsurers, all of which is catalogued in the *Handbook on Insurance Coverage Disputes* (Wolters Kluwar 2012, Sixteenth Edition).[4]

Legal Issues or Conflicts That Arise in the Area of Reinsurance

I represent insurers and reinsurers with respect to disputes that arise from time to time, as well as policy construction issues. I find that the practice of insurance and reinsurance law is extremely stimulating because there are always novel fact patterns relating to what constitutes a covered occurrence, how many occurrences there are, how insurance and reinsurance should be allocated for purposes of insurance and reinsurance purposes, and whether particular events are or are not covered by particular policy language. An almost limitless number of issues can arise out of insurance and reinsurance relationships.

Fortunately, I do not think that fraud is prevalent in the reinsurance area. Reinsurance has long been described as an honorable arrangement, and with rare exceptions, participants to reinsurance arrangements deal with each other in good faith and make appropriate disclosures.

[3] *U.S. Fid. & Guar. Co. v. Am. Reinsurance Co.*, 985 N.E.2d 876 (N.Y. 2013).
[4] Ostrager & Newman, *supra* note 1.

Over the last five years, there have been some disputes relating to the appropriateness of disclosures, as well as disputes relating to the allocation of losses to particular policy years or treaties. We have also seen issues relating to whether settlements qualify for treatment under the Follow the Fortunes Doctrine, and issues relating to potential coverage gaps that direct insurers or insureds may or may not create.

Key Aspects of Processing a Reinsurance Claim

Reinsurance transactions are transactions that are engaged in by sophisticated actors on both sides—i.e., a direct insurer knows exactly what risk the insurer wishes to reinsure, and the reinsurer understands the coverage it is providing. Of course, a reinsurer would want to know all relevant information about a claim or settlement. Damages might be determined by a jury in an actual trial or by a judge, or there may be a consensual settlement between a direct insurer and its policyholders.

Typically, the most challenging issue for direct insurers that purchase reinsurance relates to long-tail liabilities—that is, where an insured has a loss that spans many years and that loss is allocated among multiple insurers. Ultimately, the insurers that have incurred the loss seek to secure reinsurance coverage for those losses, and there may be issues relating to how these types of losses are appropriately allocated. Generally speaking, insurers and reinsurers set up a protocol for the reporting of claims or losses on a quarterly or annual basis, and that is a relatively informal arrangement.

Settlement Versus Litigation of Claims

When I am representing a direct insurer, I want to first ascertain if a particular claim is, in fact, covered by the direct insurance policy. If it is, I tend to resolve it on the best available terms on a consensual basis. If there is a coverage issue, there may be insurance coverage litigation, and I would act on behalf of the insurer.

I do not think there is any hard and fast rule with respect to whether a reinsurance claim should be litigated or settled. If a claim is clearly covered, the best practice is for the insurer and reinsurer to resolve the claim consensually. On the other hand, if there is a serious issue as to whether the claim is covered by reinsurance, it may be necessary to deal with the dispute in the adversary system and conduct discovery. During the course of discovery, it may appear that the claim is or is not covered. If the claim is not covered, the reinsurer will likely want to seek adjudication that there is no coverage.

Again, all manner of disputes may arise in this area, including whether the underlying claim is covered in the first instance and therefore covered by the reinsurance treaty, whether the claim was resolved in good faith, and whether the claim has been properly allocated to a particular policy year. As noted, the most common disputes relate to the scope of coverage provided by the reinsurance contract.

Handling Reinsurance Disputes/Litigation

When handling reinsurance disputes in this area, it is important to learn all of the relevant and material facts about the dispute and then attempt to resolve it either consensually or, depending on the facts, through litigation or arbitration. It is also important to follow the applicable rules for the conduct of the litigation or arbitration process.

When working with opposing counsel during the litigation process, you need to keep in mind that the lawyers on both sides have a duty of candor. Hopefully the lawyers who are litigating these matters will act in a professional and courteous manner; I always try to do so when dealing with opposing counsel.

Various issues are negotiated during reinsurance litigation, including the scope of discovery, the nature of discovery, the documents and witnesses that should be the subject of pre-trial discovery, and ultimately scheduling and everything antecedent to a hearing on the merits.

Obstacles that are commonly encountered in the dispute resolution process include unrealistic expectations by one or both parties in terms of how the litigation or arbitration should be resolved. Also, the opposing party or counsel may be unnecessarily difficult. Theoretically, an alternate dispute resolution process such as mediation is less expensive and faster than litigation or arbitration.

Conclusion: Upcoming Changes in Reinsurance Law/Advice for Attorneys

I do not anticipate any major changes in reinsurance law in the coming year. As noted, reinsurance arrangements—however they evolve—are arrangements between sophisticated parties who often have long experience with one another, and there is a fairly well-developed body of jurisprudence that controls the relationship between cedents and reinsurers.

I think it is important for practitioners who handle reinsurance cases to be fully conversant with the controlling legal principles, which are well documented in the literature in this area. Ultimately, to the extent that potential litigants are reasonable and responsible, any disputes can typically be resolved without full-blown litigation.

Key Takeaways

- Ascertain if a particular reinsurance claim is, in fact, covered by the direct insurance policy. Learn all of the relevant and material facts about a particular dispute and then attempt to resolve it either consensually or, depending on the facts, through litigation or arbitration. Follow the applicable rules for the conduct of the litigation or arbitration process.
- Keep in mind that the lawyers on both sides have a duty of candor and should act in a professional and courteous manner. Be prepared to negotiate various issues during reinsurance litigation, including the scope of discovery, the nature of discovery, the documents and witnesses that have to be subject to pre-trial discovery, and ultimately scheduling and everything antecedent to a hearing on the merits.
- Try to manage unrealistic expectations by one or both parties in terms of how the litigation or arbitration will be resolved. Note that, theoretically, an alternate dispute resolution process such as mediation is less expensive and faster than litigation or arbitration.

- Be fully conversant with the controlling legal principles in reinsurance cases, which are well documented in the literature in this area. To the extent that the potential litigants are reasonable and responsible, any disputes can typically be resolved without full-blown litigation.

Barry R. Ostrager is a partner at Simpson Thacher & Bartlett LLP and former chair of Simpson Thacher's Litigation Department from 1999 to 2011. He has successfully tried to verdict five cases in which more than a billion dollars were at issue. He has also successfully tried dozens of other cases to verdict and argued scores of appeals throughout the country. He has been prominently involved in the trials of many high-profile securities, antitrust, insurance, and other commercial cases. He was lead trial counsel for Swiss Re in the highly publicized insurance coverage dispute involving the World Trade Center tragedy, which resulted in a unanimous jury verdict in favor of Swiss Re, and lead counsel for Hanwha in a multibillion-dollar dispute with the Korean government that was the subject of a multi-week trial. He successfully argued before the US Supreme Court the closely followed Epstein v. Matsushita *case that arose out of Matsushita's successful tender offer for MCA Inc. In 2010, he successfully argued again before the Supreme Court the* Travelers v. Bailey *case, which resolved important issues relating to the rights of settling insurers in asbestos-related bankruptcy. He also successfully represented Andersen Consulting against a $14 billion claim by Arthur Andersen in connection with Andersen Consulting's successful bid to win a separation without cost from the Andersen Worldwide organization in the largest ICC arbitration in history.*

Recently Mr. Ostrager's trial victories have included a $110 million jury verdict for Gray Development Group in Arizona state court related to failed efforts to develop a forty-one-acre apartment complex in Phoenix, and a $30 million jury award on behalf of a member of the Jordanian Royal Family in Florida state court with respect to a commercial dispute against his former partners. Last year, he prevailed on behalf of Travelers in an insurance coverage trial he conducted in California Superior Court against Plant Insulation Company, a former Travelers insured, which was seeking limitless coverage from Travelers for asbestos personal injury claims.

Mr. Ostrager has been prominently involved in supervising the firm's major insurance and reinsurance practices in both its New York and Los Angeles offices. He has been lead trial counsel in more than a dozen major insurance coverage cases, including Shell Oil Co. v. Winterthur Swiss Insurance Company, *a multibillion-dollar environmental insurance coverage dispute in which the jury returned a verdict for the insurers after a sixteen-month trial.*

Recent Trends in Federal Court Reinsurance Litigation

Jennifer K. Gust

Partner

Hinshaw & Culbertson LLP

ASPATORE

Introduction: Reinsurance Arbitration Disputes within the Federal Courts

Reinsurance is a type of insurance commonly purchased by insurance companies from one or more other insurance or reinsurance companies to manage risk. Nearly all insurance companies enter into reinsurance agreements. By entering into reinsurance agreements to pass along risk to one or more insurers, the primary insurance carrier can issue policies with higher limits to its customers and still remain within the solvency margins established by each state's insurance regulations. Moreover, by purchasing reinsurance, an insurance company has additional flexibility to underwrite new business, which may not be otherwise possible without obtaining additional capital. By containing certain risks and passing along other risks to reinsurers, an insurance company's losses become more stable and predictable.

More often than not, reinsurance agreements include provisions that set forth how the parties to the agreement will handle disputes. Increasingly, these disputes are heard through an arbitration tribunal as opposed to state or federal courts and may be governed by the Federal Arbitration Act. Historically, arbitration has been a less expensive and more expedient method of resolving disputes. Arbitration proceedings are generally less formal and do not limit discovery based on rules of evidence unless specifically ordered by the arbitrator. Additionally, the parties to an arbitration generally have the ability to select arbitrators who have more expertise with reinsurance matters than sitting judges. Notably, the findings and evidence in an arbitration proceeding, unlike litigated matters in court, are not disclosed in the public record so that the parties may maintain confidentiality over the disputed subject matter.

However, arbitration also triggers certain disadvantages compared to traditional litigation. If a party to the arbitration is dissatisfied with the arbitrators' ruling, traditionally that party does not have a right to appeal that decision. Additionally, if the dispute involves issues concerning non-parties to the agreement, generally those non-parties cannot be compelled to arbitrate. Because arbitrated matters are administered outside of the formal court system, the parties cannot rely upon substantive precedent to gauge how an arbitration panel might rule on a particular legal issue. Finally, arbitration may not save costs or legal fees where a large amount of discovery is necessary to resolve the dispute.

This chapter addresses the most current trends in reinsurance disputes in the federal court system. Because most reinsurance contracts mandate that disputes shall be addressed in arbitration, a vast majority of the recent federal court decisions, unsurprisingly, deal with the scope and breadth of those arbitration agreements. Not only have litigants sought the assistance of the federal courts in interpreting and enforcing their respective arbitration agreements, but they have also sought direction as to whether the orders issued by arbitrators are, themselves, subject to arbitration.

Determination of the Appropriate Forum for Interpreting Arbitration Orders

The question as to the proper forum for interpreting an arbitration order was addressed in *Employers Insurance Company of Wausau v. OneBeacon America Insurance Company.*[1] The single issue presented in that case is whether an arbitrator or the federal court has the authority to determine the preclusive effect of a confirmation of an arbitration decision on subsequent arbitration actions. Is a federal judgment confirming an arbitration award separate and distinct from the arbitration award itself? The First Circuit determined it is. Under the Federal Arbitration Act (FAA),[2] a federal court's review of an arbitration decision is strictly limited to whether the arbitration decision should be vacated or amended on specific grounds listed in the act.[3] Additionally, a federal court review can provide the mechanism to enforce an arbitration decision.

Applying a collateral estoppel analysis to a federal court's review of an arbitration decision requires an analysis of the details of the prior arbitration; however, since a federal confirmation of an arbitration award does not delve into the background facts and merit of an arbitration decision, a determination of the preclusive effect of that decision generally exceeds the scope of the federal court's review. Therefore, the court held

---

[1] *Emp'rs Ins. Co. of Wausau v. OneBeacon Am. Ins. Co.*, 744 F.3d 25 (1st Cir. 2014).
[2] Federal Arbitration Act, Pub.L. 68–401, 43 Stat. 883 (1925) (codified at 9 U.S.C. §§ 1-16).
[3] *Id.*

that the preclusive effect and scope of an arbitration award, even those awards confirmed by federal courts, remain arbitrable issues.

The rule of law presented by *Wausau*[4] was later confirmed in *Liberty Mutual Insurance Company v. Allstate Insurance Company*.[5] In that case, the district court held that any issues pertaining to the interpretation, application, and performance of an arbitration order issued by a panel are, themselves, arbitrable. Liberty Mutual attempted to distinguish the *Wausau*[6] decision based on Liberty Mutual's request pertaining to the enforcement of declaratory relief; however, the district court was not persuaded, holding the broad scope of the arbitration agreement between the parties allowed for arbitration of any declaratory judgment relief in addition to the interpretation and scope of the arbitration order.

Court Power to Consolidate Arbitration Called into Question

Other district courts have been called upon to define the courts' power to consolidate arbitration actions and determine the venue of arbitration actions where the contracts are silent regarding those issues. For example, *Georgia Casualty & Surety Company v. Excalibur Reinsurance Corporation*[7] involved disputes arising from two reinsurance contracts implicated when a Georgia Casualty insured was found liable in tort after a jury trial. As a result of the underlying litigation, Georgia Casualty accrued $3 million in indemnity and $2,641,692 in litigation expenses. Georgia Casualty sought reimbursement of more than $1.4 million from Excalibur based on the reinsurance contracts between the parties. One reinsurance contract contained a choice of law provision, but no forum selection clause. The other reinsurance contract contained the opposite. When Excalibur refused to pay the amount requested, Georgia Casualty sought arbitration for breach of the agreements. Excalibur counterclaimed for arbitration on the issue of unpaid premiums. While both parties agreed to arbitrate, Excalibur refused to consolidate the arbitrations. As a result, Georgia Casualty filed suit requesting the district court to issue an order for the parties to

[4] *Emp'rs Ins. Co. of Wausau*, 744 F.3d 25 (1st Cir. 2014).
[5] *Liberty Mutual Ins. Co. v. Allstate Ins. Co.*, No. 13-cv-10387, 2014 WL 1289469 (D. Mass. Mar. 31, 2014).
[6] *Emp'rs Ins. Co. of Wausau*, 744 F.3d 25 (1st Cir. 2014).
[7] *Ga. Cas. & Sur. Co. v. Exclaibur Reinsurance Corp.*, No. 1:13-cv-00456-JEC, 2014 WL 996388 (N.D. Ga. Mar. 13, 2014).

participate in a consolidated arbitration in Atlanta; Excalibur to post security sufficient to cover the claimed losses, since rumors existed that Excalibur was approaching insolvency; and the court to stay further proceedings pending arbitration.

A district court may compel the arbitration of two separate disputes into a single arbitration proceeding under two conditions. If the FAA or a state arbitration act lacking a consolidation provision applies, a court may consolidate the arbitrations if the contracts expressly allow consolidation. If the state arbitration act allows consolidation regardless of the contract terms, a court may order consolidation. In the *Georgia Casualty*[8] case, because one of the contracts was governed by the FAA[9] and the other contract was governed by Missouri law (which does not allow courts to force consolidation), the district court held that the actions could not be consolidated.

With respect to the question as to whether the district court could order the arbitrators to stay or not to stay a particular proceeding, the district court held the court had no power over the arbitrators to stay any proceedings pending the resolution of claims against a third party because of the broad scope of the arbitration agreement. The decision to stay or not to stay particular proceedings falls within the purview of arbitration.

The district court also analyzed the plaintiff's request to force the defendant to post a security bond, which was styled as a request for injunctive relief. With respect to this issue, the district court held the plaintiff's request failed to meet the standards required to obtain equitable relief since the plaintiff was truly seeking monetary damages in the form of reimbursement from the reinsurance carrier pursuant to the contract.

Determining the Effect of Contractual Silence Regarding Pre-Judgment Interest

In one interesting recent decision, a district court was called upon to determine what effect a reinsurance contract's silence on a particular issue

[8] *Ga. Cas. & Sur. Co*, 2014 WL 996388.

[9] Federal Arbitration Act, Pub.L. 68–401, 43 Stat. 883 (1925) (codified at 9 U.S.C. §§ 1-16).

signified. Specifically, if an agreement is silent as to whether a party is entitled to pre-judgment interest on a disputed claim, did the parties intend to follow statutory law in the forum regarding pre-judgment interest, or did the parties intend to preclude the prevailing party from seeking and obtaining pre-judgment interest? This exact issue was addressed in *In re Liquidation of the Home Insurance Company.*[10]

As a point of reference, Home Insurance Company was declared insolvent and placed in liquidation in 2003. Century Indemnity Company reinsured Home with respect to certain contracts between Home and other insurers. In a previous decision, the Supreme Court of New Hampshire held that an $8 million setoff claim by Century was impermissible under New Hampshire law. After Century paid the previously withheld $8 million to the liquidator, the trial court issued a finding that Home was entitled to statutory pre-judgment interest on the $8 million, accruing from the date of the letter from the liquidator to Century disallowing the setoff. Century disagreed, arguing the pre-judgment interest statute should not apply because it was not an action of a debt or account as required by the statute, and the agreements between Century and Home do not allow for a pre-judgment interest award on a disputed setoff claim. The court held no distinction existed between an action on a disputed setoff and an action on a debt or account stated. The fact the case involved a disputed claim in liquidation rather than a lawsuit to collect a debt was inconsequential.

With respect to the award for pre-judgment interest, Century argued because the agreements between Century and Home were silent on the issue of pre-judgment interest, the parties did not intend for pre-judgment interest to apply. The court disagreed, finding the default rules pertaining to pre-judgment interest as provided by statute filled the gap in the parties' agreement. The court held that the purpose behind pre-judgment interest is to compensate a creditor for the delay between when money is due and when it is paid. Additionally, the court did not find merit in Century's argument that the agreements between the parties were "comprehensive." Rather, because several provisions within the agreement allow the parties to reserve rights against each other with respect to certain issues, and state-

[10] *In re Liquidation of Home Ins. Co.*, 89 A.3d 165 (N.H. 2014).

disputed claims are within the purview of New Hampshire statutory law, the parties demonstrated intent to apply statutory law when necessary.

Exploring the Ramifications of Unspecific Arbitrators' Orders

One district court was called upon to determine the ramifications of an arbitrator's order that provided a general framework for relief, but did not assign a specific amount in damages. The decision in *R&Q Reinsurance Company v. Utica Mutual Insurance Company*[11] contemplates whether an order issued by an arbitration panel that provides a conceptual framework for payment of an award instead of an exact dollar amount constitutes a final and enforceable order. In this case, R&Q and Utica sought arbitration to resolve the amount R&Q owed to Utica for billings arising out of nine reinsurance certificates pertaining to asbestos-related losses suffered by Utica-insured Goulds Pumps Inc. Utica's billings to R&Q fell into four categories: (1) indemnity payments, (2) defense costs, (3) orphan shares, and (4) declaratory judgment expenses. The arbitration panel was tasked with determining which of these categories Utica could recover from R&Q. "Orphan shares" refers to amounts that Utica would have billed to Goulds or Goulds' other insurers, but that have become uncollectible (usually because of insolvency). Utica sought to reallocate these costs to reinsurers, including R&Q.

After a seven-day evidentiary hearing and extended briefing, the panel determined the policies issued by Utica to Goulds had aggregate limits of $500,000 each. Additionally, the panel held the reinsurance certificates do not cover defense costs, orphan shares, declaratory judgment expenses, attorneys' fees, costs, or interest. The panel did not, however, make a determination of the exact amount R&Q owed Utica. After Utica filed several unsuccessful motions for reconsideration and/or clarification with the panel, R&Q filed a petition to confirm the arbitration award in federal court.

Arbitration awards are not self-enforcing, but the FAA[12] provides a mechanism for parties to seek confirmation or move to vacate, modify,

[11] *R&Q Reinsurance Co. v. Utica Mut. Ins. Co.*, No. 13 Civ. 8013(PAE), 2014 WL 584309 (S.D.N.Y. Feb. 14, 2014).

[12] Federal Arbitration Act.

or correct an award. Review of that award by a district court is severely limited so as to avoid having the parties essentially litigate the case for a second time. The prevailing opinion is that an arbitration award should be enforced, even if the court disagrees with the award on its merits, if there is even the slightest justification for the decision reached. The Southern District of New York determined that even though the arbitration panel did not issue an award in terms of specific dollar amounts, the award itself did constitute a final order. The parties had presented the case to the panel in a conceptual manner without directly addressing specific amounts owed. Therefore, the panel issued its decision in a conceptual manner that provided a framework for payment on past due amounts and future amounts owed for the continuing asbestos losses. Unhappy the award did not provide any compensation for defense costs or orphan shares as part of the overall scheme, Utica attempted to force the panel and the district court to revisit this issue to recover additional dollars. Utica's attempt to get a second bite at the apple failed, and the district court determined the arbitration panel's ruling constituted a final order.

This case certainly represents a situation in which a party must be careful what it asks for with respect to the framework of its argument and its request for relief. Having presented the case in front of the arbitration panel in a general conceptual manner, Utica should not have been surprised when the order issued by the arbitration panel mirrored the categories presented by the parties.

Pre-Pleading Security Issues Examined

In another recent decision, *Travelers Indemnity Co v. Excalibur Reinsurance Corporation*,[13] a district court was posed with an issue relating to the posting of security bonds. Specifically, this case answers the question regarding whether a company that cancels its authorization to do business in a particular state may avoid posting pre-pleading security if the change in status is made after the parties sign the reinsurance treaty at issue. The analysis undertaken by the district court involved a comparison of Rule

[13] *Travelers Indem. Co. v. Excalibur Reinsurance Corp.*, No. 3:11-CV-1209 (CSH), 2014 WL 941444 (D. Conn. Mar. 11, 2014).

64,[14] the choice of law analysis under *Erie*,[15] and the contractual choice of law agreed to by the parties.

Under Federal Rule 64(a),[16] "at the commencement of and throughout an action, every remedy is available that, under the law of the state where the court is located, provides for seizing a person or property to secure satisfaction of the potential judgment. But a federal statute governs to the extent that it applies." The initial question is whether the laws referenced in Rule 64(a)[17] also include the state's choice of law principles.

The district court analyzed the available cases interpreting Rule 64[18] and determined the rule did not preclude the application of the forum state's choice of law rules or the application of the pre-pleading security statute. The *Erie*[19] analysis conducted on the facts of the case yielded the same result. Because the pre-pleading security statute was categorized as procedural as opposed to substantive, the rules of the forum state, including the pre-pleading security statute, applied. The district court held that under either scenario, any insurance company that decides for whatever reason to withdraw its authorization to do business in a particular state will face the consequences of that decision, including posting pre-pleading security.

In essence, this decision reinforces the public policy behind the enforcement of remedies available in a forum state against insurance companies. In this instance, the consequence of a reinsurer's failure to post security under the state statute is to strike the reinsurer's answer and enter judgment in favor of the insurer. If an insurance carrier chooses to deauthorize its ability to do business in a particular state, that insurer must be willing to post adequate security in any subsequent litigation or face court sanctions.

---

[14] Fed. R. Civ. P. 64.
[15] *Erie R. Co. v. Tompkins*, 304 U.S. 64 (1938).
[16] Fed. R. Civ. P. 64(a).
[17] Fed. R. Civ. P. 64(a).
[18] Fed. R. Civ. P. 64.
[19] *Erie R. Co.*, 304 U.S. 64 (1938).

Conclusion

Considering the present economic climate and the volatility of the insurance industry as a whole, insurance carriers can expect an expansion of litigation in the reinsurance arena, which, more often than not, will be addressed through the arbitration process. As the litigated issues become increasingly complex, insurance carriers and practitioners can expect the district courts to continue expanding the scope and power of arbitration panels involved in reinsurance disputes to assist the adjudication of these issues in an expedient manner.

Consequently, as a reinsurance practitioner, it is important to consider the impact of arbitration on your insurance client's litigated disputes. Where the reinsurance agreement mandates arbitration of all disputes, it is important to communicate to your client that, more often than not, any dissatisfaction with a panel's ruling will have to be addressed through arbitration, and not through the court system. Because arbitrated matters are confidential and do not establish precedent or rule of law, the chance of success associated with any particular dispute can be difficult to predict.

Additionally, when entering into the arbitration process, it is important to select arbitrators who are experienced in complex reinsurance matters, even if those individuals would cost more to retain. Because arbitrated matters are generally not subject to appeal, it is imperative that you select arbitrators on the panel who have the experience and legal ability to render your client a well-reasoned outcome.

Key Takeaways

- Because most reinsurance contracts require disputes to be addressed in arbitration, a vast majority of the recent federal court decisions deal with the scope and breadth of those arbitration agreements.
- Under the FAA,[20] a federal court's review of an arbitration decision is strictly limited to whether the arbitration decision should be vacated or amended on specific grounds listed in the act.[21]

[20] Federal Arbitration Act, Pub.L. 68–401, 43 Stat. 883 (1925) (codified at 9 U.S.C. §§ 1-16).
[21] *Id.*

Additionally, a federal court review can provide the mechanism to enforce an arbitration decision.

- Arbitration awards are not self-enforcing, but the FAA[22] provides a mechanism for parties to seek confirmation or move to vacate, modify, or correct an award. The prevailing opinion is that an arbitration award should be enforced, even if the court disagrees with the award on its merits, if there is even the slightest justification for the decision reached.
- The scope and interpretation of arbitration awards and opinions issued during the arbitration process are also subject to arbitration and are generally outside of the domain of the court system.
- If an insurance carrier chooses to deauthorize its ability to do business in a particular state, the insurer must be willing to post adequate security in any subsequent litigation or face court sanctions.

Jennifer K. Gust, a partner with Hinshaw & Culbertson LLP, specializes in litigating complex business disputes representing insurance and financial industry clients. She excels at leading litigation teams, counseling clients, providing risk management services, and drafting opinion letters involving breach of contract, Uniform Commercial Code, Fair Credit Reporting Act, Electronic Funds Transfer Act, Telephone Consumer Protection Act, commercial liability, personal/advertising injury, directors and officers/errors and omissions, professional lines, reinsurance, and excess coverages.

Ms. Gust is a prolific speaker, published author, and advocate regarding substantive legal issues and women's professional development in Chicago's legal community. Currently, she serves as a member of the Board of Directors of the Coalition of Women's Initiatives in Law and the Illinois Association of Defense Trial Counsel.

---

[22] *Id.*

Developments in the Regulation of Reinsurance in the United States

Leah Campbell and Donald B. Henderson Jr.

Partners

Willkie Farr & Gallagher LLP

ASPATORE

Introduction

There are two ongoing developments in the regulation of reinsurance in the United States that are of broad interest. One is the adoption by the National Association of Insurance Commissioners (NAIC) and a growing number of states of new rules that permit non-US reinsurers to qualify for reduced levels of collateral to secure their obligations to US cedents. The second is a review by the NAIC and certain state regulators of life insurers' reinsurance arrangements with captive insurance companies. We discuss below in order these two recent developments.

Under the US regulatory scheme, US insurance companies are generally free to purchase reinsurance from any reinsurer of their choosing, and on whatever terms they negotiate. However, certain criteria must be met for a US cedent to reflect reinsurance as an asset on its statutory financial statements or, alternatively, to reduce reserves to reflect the reinsurance. This financial statement treatment is known as "credit for reinsurance." The failure of reinsurance to qualify for credit for reinsurance results in adverse accounting for the cedent. For this reason, cedents have a strong incentive to comply with the rules governing credit for reinsurance.

Credit for Reinsurance Rules

NAIC Model Credit for Reinsurance Act and Regulation

The NAIC's model act and regulation on credit for reinsurance (the "Model Law")[1] is in effect in some form in each of the fifty states and the District of Columbia.[2] Under the federal Dodd–Frank Wall Street Reform and Consumer Protection Act, the regulation of reinsurance is solely within the purview of the state of domicile of the cedent.[3] Under the Model Law, provided the reinsurance agreement includes certain prescribed terms, the

---

[1] *See* NAIC, Credit for Reinsurance Model Insurance Law (2012), *available at* www.naic.org/store/free/MDL-785.pdf; *see also* NAIC, Credit for Reinsurance Model Insurance Regulation (2012), *available at* www.naic.org/store/free/MDL-786.pdf.

[2] The NAIC Model Law on Credit for Reinsurance and the NAIC Credit for Reinsurance Model Regulation are part of the NAIC accreditation standards for the states. NAIC, Financial Regulation Standards and Accreditation Program 10 (2014).

[3] 15 U.S.C. § 8221(b).

cedent may take reinsurance credit for the obligations of the reinsurer as an asset or as a reduction of liabilities if the reinsurer:

1. Maintains a license in the cedent's state of domicile;
2. Is an accredited reinsurer in the state of domicile of the cedent, meaning the regulators in such state have formally approved the reinsurer for credit for reinsurance purposes;
3. Is domiciled in a state that has credit for reinsurance requirements substantially similar to those of the cedent's state of domicile;
4. Is a group including incorporated and individual unincorporated underwriters (e.g., Lloyd's) (which is required to maintain (a) a trust fund in an amount not less than the group's several liabilities attributable to business ceded by US cedents to any member of the group pursuant to reinsurance contracts issued in the name of the group, and (b) a joint trusteed surplus of which $100 million for the benefit of US cedents of any member of the group);
5. Is a group of incorporated underwriters under common administration (e.g., the Institute of London Underwriters) that maintains the requisite policyholders' surplus and a trust fund in the requisite amount for the benefit of US cedents;
6. Maintains a multi-beneficiary trust for the benefit of its US cedents, with funds equal to its liabilities to US cedents plus the requisite trusteed surplus amount, subject to the approval of the regulators of the cedent's state of domicile;
7. Establishes a single beneficiary trust for the benefit of the cedent that meets the requirements of the credit for reinsurance laws of the state of domicile; or
8. Posts a letter of credit for the benefit of the cedent that meets the requirements for credit for reinsurance under the laws of the cedent's state of domicile.[4]

Under the Model Law, unless the reinsurer is a "certified reinsurer" entitled to establish a reduced level of reinsurance collateral, a reinsurer that establishes collateral in the United States pursuant to items 7 or 8 above, is required to fund the trust account or letter of credit in an amount equal to 100 percent of the reinsurer's obligations to the US

[4] NAIC Credit for Reinsurance Model Law 785 § 2 (2012).

cedent.[5] In addition, a certified reinsurer that establishes a multi-beneficiary trust pursuant to item 6 above is permitted to reduce the amount maintained in the trust account to equal the permitted lower percentage of its obligations to US cedents, plus the requisite trusteed surplus amount. Some of the statutory requirements for a single beneficiary trust and for a letter of credit are set forth below.

Single Beneficiary Trust

1. The trust agreement must be entered into among the cedent (as beneficiary), the reinsurer (as grantor), and a trustee that is a qualified US financial institution.
2. The beneficiary must have the unrestricted right to withdraw assets from the trust account upon written notice only to the trustee (a requirement that prior notice be given to the grantor is prohibited).
3. In general, the trust agreement cannot refer to any other agreement or be subject to any external conditions or requirements.
4. The trust agreement must be established for the sole benefit of the beneficiary.
5. The trust agreement must require the trustee to determine that all assets are in such form that the beneficiary (or the trustee, upon direction by the beneficiary) may whenever necessary negotiate such assets, without consent or signature from any other person (including the grantor).
6. The trust agreement must require the trustee to furnish to the grantor and the beneficiary a statement of all assets in the trust account upon its inception and by the end of each calendar quarter.
7. The trust agreement must notify the grantor and the beneficiary within ten days of any deposits or withdrawals from the trust account.
8. The trust agreement must require the trustee, upon written demand of the beneficiary, to immediately take all steps necessary to transfer all right, title, and interest in the trust assets to the beneficiary and deliver physical custody of the assets to the beneficiary.

[5] NAIC Credit for Reinsurance Model Regulation 786 § 10(A) (2013).

9. The trust agreement must generally allow no substitutions or withdrawals of assets from the account, except on written instructions from the beneficiary.
10. The trust agreement must be made subject to and governed by the laws of the state in which the trust is domiciled.
11. The reinsurance agreement or the trust agreement must stipulate that assets deposited in the trust account must be valued according to their fair market value and must consist only of cash, certificates of deposit, and permitted investments.[6]

Letter of Credit

1. The letter of credit must be clean, irrevocable, unconditional, and issued or confirmed by a qualified US financial institution.
2. The letter of credit must contain an issue date and expiration date and stipulate that the cedent (as beneficiary) need only draw a sight draft under the letter of credit and present it to obtain funds and that no other document need be presented.
3. The letter of credit must indicate that it is not subject to any conditions or qualifications outside of the letter of credit, and generally may not contain reference to any other agreements, documents, or entities.
4. The obligation of the financial institution under the letter of credit may not be contingent upon reimbursement.
5. The term of the letter of credit must be for at least one year.
6. The letter of credit must contain an "evergreen clause," meaning it automatically renews unless prior notice is given to the beneficiary, which, at that point, may draw down the entire amount of the letter of credit.[7]

Certified Reinsurers

For many years, state insurance regulators, the NAIC, and industry participants have debated whether the 100 percent reinsurance collateral requirement applicable to non-US reinsurers imposed an unfair standard on financially strong and well-rated foreign reinsurers. In this respect, the

[6] NAIC Credit for Reinsurance Model Regulation 786 § 11 (2013).
[7] NAIC Credit for Reinsurance Model Regulation 786 § 12 (2013).

foreign reinsurance market argued that US-licensed reinsurers with questionable capital and poor ratings were not required to secure their reinsurance obligations to US cedents, thereby posing a significant financial risk to such cedents. On the other hand, highly capitalized and rated non-US reinsurers were always required to completely secure their obligations to US cedents. The US reinsurance market generally argued that the 100 percent collateral requirement was necessary because non-US reinsurers are not regulated in the United States and in the absence of full collateral maintained in a qualified US financial institution, a non-US reinsurer could refuse or fail to pay valid claims, resulting in the US cedent having to secure payment through legal proceedings initiated in jurisdictions around the world. In November 2011, the NAIC adopted amendments to the Model Law establishing the concept of a "certified reinsurer" that would be entitled to reduced collateral standards subject to specific requirements. A summary of the certified reinsurer amendments to the Model Law and the processing of certified reinsurer applications is set forth below.

Standards for Certified Reinsurer Status

The NAIC and a growing number of states have adopted new rules pursuant to which a US cedent may receive full credit for the reinsurance obligations of a qualifying non-US reinsurer (i.e., a "certified reinsurer") based on reduced (i.e., less than 100 percent) collateral posted by such reinsurer.[8] Under the Model Law, reinsurers domiciled in countries determined to have strong systems of domestic insurance regulation (i.e., "qualified jurisdictions") are eligible to apply for "certified reinsurer" status in states that have adopted the amendments.[9] In addition, to qualify as a certified reinsurer, an applicant must meet the following criteria as to financial strength and reliability:

1. Maintain capital and surplus of at least $250 million
2. Maintain financial strength ratings from two or more acceptable rating agencies

[8] *See, e.g.*, NAIC Credit for Reinsurance Model Law 785 § 2(E) (2012); NAIC Credit for Reinsurance Model Regulation 786 § 8 (2013); N.Y. Comp. Codes R. & Regs. tit. 11 § 125.4(h).

[9] These states are: Alabama, California, Connecticut, Delaware, Florida, Georgia, Indiana, Iowa, Louisiana, Maine, Maryland, Missouri, New Hampshire, New Jersey, New Mexico, New York, Pennsylvania, Rhode Island, and Virginia.

3. Agree to post 100 percent security upon the entry of an order of rehabilitation, liquidation, or conservation against the cedent
4. Comply with related requirements[10]

Key Procedural Elements of the Certified Reinsurer Determination

1. A state will evaluate a reinsurer that applies for certification, and will assign a rating based on the evaluation. A certified reinsurer will be required to post collateral in an amount that corresponds with its assigned rating (0 percent, 10 percent, 20 percent, 50 percent, 75 percent, or 100 percent), for a US cedent to be allowed full financial statement credit for the reinsurance ceded.[11]
2. Each state will have the authority to certify reinsurers, or a state insurance commissioner may recognize the certification issued by another NAIC-accredited state.[12]
3. The NAIC will publish a list of qualified non-US jurisdictions. State insurance commissioners must document any reasons for approving a jurisdiction not on this list.[13]
4. A US cedent is required to notify its domestic regulator if reinsurance ceded to an individual reinsurer or group of affiliated reinsurers exceeds certain specified amounts.[14]
5. A certified reinsurer is required to provide certain information to the certifying state upon becoming a certified reinsurer, and annually thereafter.[15]

Qualified Non-US Jurisdictions

The Model Law provides that to be eligible for certification and collateral reduction, among other things, a non-US reinsurer must be domiciled and licensed to transact insurance or reinsurance in a "qualified jurisdiction."[16] State insurance commissioners are responsible for determining whether the reinsurer's domiciliary jurisdiction is

[10] NAIC Credit for Reinsurance Model Law 785 § 2 (2012).
[11] NAIC Credit for Reinsurance Model Regulation 786 § 8(A) (2013).
[12] NAIC Credit for Reinsurance Model Regulation 786 §§ 8(A), (D) (2013).
[13] NAIC Credit for Reinsurance Model Regulation 786 § 8(C) (2013)
[14] NAIC Credit for Reinsurance Model Law 785 § 2(J) (2012).
[15] NAIC Credit for Reinsurance Model Regulation 786 § 8(B)(7) (2013).
[16] NAIC Credit for Reinsurance Model Law 785 § 2(E)(1)(a) (2012).

eligible to be recognized as a qualified jurisdiction, and must consider the NAIC's list of qualified jurisdictions in making this determination.[17] While not expressly stated in the Model Law, the intent is for states to be able to rely upon the NAIC's list of qualified foreign jurisdictions. Indeed, Florida's amended laws provide that the commissioner may make a determination as to a qualified foreign jurisdiction based upon the NAIC's findings.[18]

The Qualified Jurisdiction (E) Working Group, established by the NAIC to allow those states that have adopted the Model Law to implement reduced collateral requirements, has assigned the "Conditional Qualified Jurisdiction" designation to the international supervisory authorities of Bermuda (Bermuda Monetary Authority), Germany (German Federal Financial Supervisory Authority), Switzerland (Swiss Financial Market Supervisory Authority), and the United Kingdom (Prudential Regulation Authority of the Bank of England). The Working Group intends to complete its full evaluation procedure for these four jurisdictions in 2014. The approval of these four countries, which represent a significant share of the reinsurance market, as Conditional Qualified Jurisdictions permits qualified reinsurers that are domiciled and licensed to transact insurance or reinsurance in such jurisdictions to post reduced collateral amounts for the benefit of US cedents. This marks a major milestone in the NAIC's implementation of the Model Law.

NAIC Support and Assistance

At the same time, the NAIC's Reinsurance (E) Financial Analysis Working Group (the "Reinsurance-FAWG"), a confidential, regulator-to-regulator-only group, has been established by the NAIC to provide advisory support and assistance to states in the review of non-US reinsurers' certified reinsurer applications. An approval, or "passporting," by the Reinsurance-FAWG signifies that the Reinsurance-FAWG agreed with, and voted to accept, the approving states' determination, and other states may now choose to rely on this assessment without having to undertake their own independent review of these reinsurers.

---

[17] NAIC Credit for Reinsurance Model Law 785 § 2(E)(3) (2012).
[18] Fla. Admin. Code Ann. r. 69O-144.007(9)(B) (2008).

To date, the Reinsurance-FAWG has reviewed and passported over twenty reinsurers that had previously been certified and eligible for collateral reductions by the states of Connecticut, Florida, or New York. Since the passported status is valid for only one year, the Reinsurance-FAWG will also be working in 2014 to develop a renewal process whereby it will review the financial condition of passported reinsurers.

Statewide implementation of the Model Law continues at a steady pace, and the NAIC remains hard at work through the qualified jurisdiction and certified reinsurer passporting process to ensure that reinsurers are able to take full advantage of the reduced collateral requirements. In the meantime, as is required by the Model Law, the reduced collateral amounts will be reexamined in 2014. In addition, the Qualified Jurisdiction (E) Working Group will be reviewing Ireland and France in 2014 for eligibility as qualified jurisdictions. Two additional, though unnamed, jurisdictions have also been invited by the Qualified Jurisdiction (E) Working Group to participate in this evaluation process.

Captive Insurance Companies

Background: Reinsurance of Life Insurers' XXX and A-XXX Reserves

States have, for many years, permitted captive insurance companies to be formed for specific purposes. Historically, they have been formed to insure (or reinsure) the risks of their owner or owners. Owners were typically large business enterprises or associations of business enterprises. Since captives only insure (or reinsure) risks of their owners, they are not subject to the full range of regulation applicable to regular insurance companies. Starting in 2002, life insurance companies began to look at the captive laws as ways to finance reserves resulting from level premium term life products ("XXX" reserves) and from universal life products with secondary guarantees ("A-XXX" reserves). The XXX reserves result from the feature of the term products that provide a level premium for a specified number of years. The A-XXX reserves result from the feature of the universal life products that guarantee the policy will not lapse if a specified amount of premium is paid.

The motivation for wanting to finance XXX and A-XXX reserves is the level of reserves prescribed under statutory accounting for these products. Many industry members and consulting actuaries are of the view that the reserves are too high, and indeed they exceed the reserves prescribed under US GAAP accounting.

Starting in May 2003, life insurers (or their affiliates) began to form captives to reinsure the level premium term and/or universal life with secondary guaranty risks of the insurer. The first captives were formed in South Carolina, and later captives were formed in Vermont and elsewhere for this purpose.

Credit for Reinsurance Issues

The initial captive arrangements were designed to comply with the credit for reinsurance rules and did not attract very much regulatory criticism. Under the initial model, a life insurer formed the captive and provided initial capitalization. The captive then issued surplus notes to a special-purpose vehicle that, in turn, issued its own notes to investors. The special-purpose vehicle notes were guaranteed by one of the major financial guaranty companies and were rated AAA. The captive then entered into a reinsurance agreement with the sponsoring life insurer. The life insurer paid a reinsurance premium equal to the reserves that its actuaries and the financial guaranty company agreed were adequate to support the risks assumed (economic reserves). The captive deposited the reinsurance premium, plus the proceeds of the issuance of the surplus notes, into a credit for reinsurance trust to fully fund the statutory reserves. Over time, investment banks came up with variations on this structure, but all were designed to comply with the credit for reinsurance rules.

During the financial crisis, the financial guaranty insurers that were involved with captive financing stopped writing new business. As a result, life insurers turned to banks to issue letters of credit to finance the statutory reserves in excess of the economic reserves (the "excess reserves"). Initially, the letters of credit complied with the credit for reinsurance rules. Over time, banks began to require that the letters of credit be subject to various conditions. These conditions included restrictions on the right to draw on the letter of credit and a definite end-date to the letter of credit. More recently, captive financing has moved to note structures that operate in a manner somewhat similar to a letter of credit, but have been provided not only by banks but also by reinsurance companies. Some states began to accept a mere guaranty by a non-insurance company parent of the life insurer as acceptable financing. The conditional letters of credit, the note structures, and the parent guarantees do not comply with the credit for reinsurance rules, but have been permitted by state regulators as part of the regulators' discretion to permit exceptions to these rules.

Regulators' Concerns

As captive financing that does not comply with the credit for reinsurance rules has become more prevalent, some regulators have been concerned about the practice. In 2012, the NAIC began a review of captive financing, which is ongoing. In June 2013, the New York Department of Financial Services issued a report on captive financing that characterized the use of captives to finance excess reserves as "shadow insurance."[19]

The NAIC review and the New York report have to be viewed in the context of another ongoing development in the NAIC, namely principle-based reserving (PBR). Under PBR, life insurance reserves would be calculated based on an analysis of the products issued by the insurer and the insurer's experience rather than on prescribed actuarial formulae. The industry hopes that PBR would result in the elimination, or at least reduction of, excess reserves. Whether PBR will be put in place is subject to some doubt. A few important states, including New York and California, are opposed to the entire concept.

Rector Report and Recommendations

In its review of captive financing, the NAIC hired Rector & Associates Inc. to issue a report on the topic. The report has gone through several drafts,

[19] New York State Department of Financial Services, *Shining a Light on Shadow Insurance* (2013), *available at* www.dfs.ny.gov/reportpub/shadow_insurance_report_2013.pdf.

but a current report[20] attempts to reconcile the credit for reinsurance rules and PBR.

The Rector report acknowledges that XXX and A-XXX reserves are perceived by many as being too high, and endorses the concept of economic reserves and excess reserves. The report goes on to recommend that economic reserves be funded with traditional investment assets and that excess reserves be permitted to be funded with other assets. In defining economic reserves, the report looks to the reserving methodologies in the proposed PBR rules. Industry commentators have observed that this approach would be a useful development, but that the PBR reserves would still be excessive. States that oppose the use of captives to finance XXX and A-XXX reserves can be expected to continue to oppose the concept. The NAIC process will likely continue for some time. Once the NAIC adopts a final position and issues guidelines for reserve financing, it will be up to each state as to whether to follow them. Nevertheless, regulators in many states will likely follow the guidelines to avoid criticism by other regulators.

Conclusion

The regulation of reinsurance in the United States continues to evolve. The certified reinsurer concept is likely to be adopted by additional states, and additional reinsurers will be recognized as such in the future. While it is difficult to predict the final result of the activity surrounding captives and PBR, it seems certain that the current reserve financing technique will change as the NAIC completes its work.

Key Takeaways

- After many years of debate, which was sometimes contentious, the US regulators are implementing a system whereby well-capitalized non-admitted reinsurers will be able to provide reinsurance to US cedents without having to provide full security for their reinsurance obligations.

---

[20] Rector & Associates Inc., Report of Rector & Associates Inc. to the Principle-Based Reserving Implementation (EX) Task Force (2014), *available at* www.naic.org/documents/committees_ex_pbr_implementation_tf_140414_report_rector.pdf.

- The NAIC and certain state regulators are reviewing the use of captive insurance companies to reinsure the risks of life insurance companies. The current structures that do not meet the credit for reinsurance rules will likely be phased out.
- Reduced collateral for certified reinsurer obligations is permitted but not required. The US cedent may negotiate for 100 percent collateral on commercial grounds.
- The NAIC and certain state regulators are reviewing the use of captive insurance companies to reinsure the risks of life insurance companies. The current structures that do not meet the credit for reinsurance rules will likely be phased out.

Leah Campbell *is a partner in Willkie Farr & Gallagher LLP's Corporate and Financial Services Department. She specializes in transactional and regulatory matters involving the insurance industry. Her experience includes mergers and acquisitions, restructurings and reorganizations, corporate governance, and regulatory compliance. She represents clients in matters before state insurance departments and provides regulatory advice in transactional contexts. She has particular experience in non-admitted insurance matters and the intersection between insurance contracts and other financial services products. She also has a significant practice representing insurance brokers, agencies, and managing underwriters on matters including compensation, referral arrangements, licensing, and general compliance.*

Donald B. Henderson Jr. *is a partner in the Corporate and Financial Services Department of Willkie Farr & Gallagher LLP. He practices in the corporate area with an emphasis on merger and acquisition transactions in the insurance industry, complex reinsurance transactions, and general corporate and regulatory matters for insurance clients. His practice includes advising clients in the purchase and sale of businesses, including both stock and asset transactions, and purchases and sales of specific blocks of business. He also advises clients in connection with alternative risk transfer arrangements, life settlements, and premium finance.*

APPENDICES

APPENDIX A

MODEL 785 S 2

Credit Allowed a Domestic Ceding Insurer

Credit for reinsurance shall be allowed a domestic ceding insurer as either an asset or a reduction from liability on account of reinsurance ceded only when the reinsurer meets the requirements of Subsections A, B, C, D, E or F of this section. Credit shall be allowed under Subsections A, B or C of this section only as respects cessions of those kinds or classes of business which the assuming insurer is licensed or otherwise permitted to write or assume in its state of domicile or, in the case of a U.S. branch of an alien assuming insurer, in the state through which it is entered and licensed to transact insurance or reinsurance. Credit shall be allowed under Subsections C or D of this section only if the applicable requirements of Subsection G have been satisfied.

A. Credit shall be allowed when the reinsurance is ceded to an assuming insurer that is licensed to transact insurance or reinsurance in this state.

   Drafting Note: A state that provides for licensing of reinsurance by line, for consistency should adopt an amended version of Subsection A requiring the assuming insurer to be "licensed to transact reinsurance in this state."

B. Credit shall be allowed when the reinsurance is ceded to an assuming insurer that is accredited by the commissioner as a reinsurer in this state. In order to be eligible for accreditation, a reinsurer must:

   1. File with the commissioner evidence of its submission to this state's jurisdiction;
   2. Submit to this state's authority to examine its books and records;
   3. Be licensed to transact insurance or reinsurance in at least one state, or in the case of a U.S. branch of an alien assuming insurer, be entered through and licensed to transact insurance or reinsurance in at least one state;

4. File annually with the commissioner a copy of its annual statement filed with the insurance department of its state of domicile and a copy of its most recent audited financial statement; and
5. Demonstrate to the satisfaction of the commissioner that it has adequate financial capacity to meet its reinsurance obligations and is otherwise qualified to assume reinsurance from domestic insurers. An assuming insurer is deemed to meet this requirement as of the time of its application if it maintains a surplus as regards policyholders in an amount not less than $20,000,000 and its accreditation has not been denied by the commissioner within ninety (90) days after submission of its application.

Drafting Note: To qualify as an accredited reinsurer, an assuming insurer must meet all of the requirements and the standards set forth in Subsection B. If the commissioner of insurance determines that the assuming insurer has failed to continue to meet any of these qualifications, the commissioner may, upon written notice and hearing, revoke accreditation.

C.

1. Credit shall be allowed when the reinsurance is ceded to an assuming insurer that is domiciled in, or in the case of a U.S. branch of an alien assuming insurer is entered through, a state that employs standards regarding credit for reinsurance substantially similar to those applicable under this statute and the assuming insurer or U.S. branch of an alien assuming insurer:

   (a) Maintains a surplus as regards policyholders in an amount not less than $20,000,000; and
   (b) Submits to the authority of this state to examine its books and records.

2. The requirement of Section 2 C(1)(a) does not apply to reinsurance ceded and assumed pursuant to pooling arrangements among insurers in the same holding company system.

Drafting Note: The term "substantially similar" means standards that equal or exceed the standards of the enacting state, as determined by the commissioner of the enacting state. It is expected that the NAIC will maintain a list of states whose laws establish standards that equal or exceed the standards of this model act.

D.

1. Credit shall be allowed when the reinsurance is ceded to an assuming insurer that maintains a trust fund in a qualified U.S. financial institution, as defined in Section 4B, for the payment of the valid claims of its U.S. ceding insurers, their assigns and successors in interest. To enable the commissioner to determine the sufficiency of the trust fund, the assuming insurer shall report annually to the commissioner information substantially the same as that required to be reported on the NAIC Annual Statement form by licensed insurers. The assuming insurer shall submit to examination of its books and records by the commissioner and bear the expense of examination.
2.

   (a) Credit for reinsurance shall not be granted under this subsection unless the form of the trust and any amendments to the trust have been approved by:

      i. The commissioner of the state where the trust is domiciled; or
      ii. The commissioner of another state who, pursuant to the terms of the trust instrument, has accepted principal regulatory oversight of the trust.

   (b) The form of the trust and any trust amendments also shall be filed with the commissioner of every state in which the ceding insurer beneficiaries of the trust are domiciled. The trust instrument shall provide that contested claims shall be valid and enforceable upon the final order of any court of competent jurisdiction in the United States. The trust shall vest legal title to its assets in its trustees for the benefit of the assuming insurer's U.S. ceding insurers, their assigns and successors in interest. The trust and the assuming insurer shall be subject to examination as determined by the commissioner.

(c) The trust shall remain in effect for as long as the assuming insurer has outstanding obligations due under the reinsurance agreements subject to the trust. No later than February 28 of each year the trustee of the trust shall report to the commissioner in writing the balance of the trust and listing the trust's investments at the preceding year-end and shall certify the date of termination of the trust, if so planned, or certify that the trust will not expire prior to the following December 31.

3. The following requirements apply to the following categories of assuming insurer:

(a) The trust fund for a single assuming insurer shall consist of funds in trust in an amount not less than the assuming insurer's liabilities attributable to reinsurance ceded by U.S. ceding insurers, and, in addition, the assuming insurer shall maintain a trusteed surplus of not less than $20,000,000, except as provided in paragraph 3(b) of this subsection.

(b) At any time after the assuming insurer has permanently discontinued underwriting new business secured by the trust for at least three full years, the commissioner with principal regulatory oversight of the trust may authorize a reduction in the required trusteed surplus, but only after a finding, based on an assessment of the risk, that the new required surplus level is adequate for the protection of U.S. ceding insurers, policyholders and claimants in light of reasonably foreseeable adverse loss development. The risk assessment may involve an actuarial review, including an independent analysis of reserves and cash flows, and shall consider all material risk factors, including when applicable the lines of business involved, the stability of the incurred loss estimates and the effect of the surplus requirements on the assuming insurer's liquidity or solvency. The minimum required trusteed surplus may not be reduced to an amount less than thirty percent (30%) of the assuming insurer's liabilities attributable to reinsurance ceded by U.S. ceding insurers covered by the trust.

(c)

i. In the case of a group including incorporated and individual unincorporated underwriters:

(I) For reinsurance ceded under reinsurance agreements with an inception, amendment or renewal date on or after January 1, 1993, the trust shall consist of a trusteed account in an amount not less than the respective underwriters' several liabilities attributable to business ceded by U.S. domiciled ceding insurers to any underwriter of the group;

(II) For reinsurance ceded under reinsurance agreements with an inception date on or before December 31, 1992, and not amended or renewed after that date, not-withstanding the other provisions of this Act, the trust shall consist of a trusteed account in an amount not less than the respective underwriters' several insurance and reinsurance liabilities attributable to business written in the United States; and

(III) In addition to these trusts, the group shall maintain in trust a trusteed surplus of which $100,000,000 shall be held jointly for the benefit of the U.S. domiciled ceding insurers of any member of the group for all years of account; and

ii. The incorporated members of the group shall not be engaged in any business other than underwriting as a member of the group and shall be subject to the same level of regulation and solvency control by the group's domiciliary regulator as are the unincorporated members.

iii. Within ninety (90) days after its financial statements are due to be filed with the group's domiciliary regulator, the group shall provide to the commissioner an annual certification by the group's domiciliary regulator of the solvency of each underwriter member; or if a certification is unavailable, financial statements, prepared by independent public accountants, of each underwriter member of the group.

(d) In the case of a group of incorporated underwriters under common administration, the group shall:

i. Have continuously transacted an insurance business outside the United States for at least three (3) years immediately prior to making application for accreditation;
ii. Maintain aggregate policyholders' surplus of at least $10,000,000,000;
iv. Maintain a trust fund in an amount not less than the group's several liabilities attributable to business ceded by U.S. domiciled ceding insurers to any member of the group pursuant to reinsurance contracts issued in the name of the group;
v. In addition, maintain a joint trusteed surplus of which $100,000,000 shall be held jointly for the benefit of U.S. domiciled ceding insurers of any member of the group as additional security for these liabilities; and
vi. Within ninety (90) days after its financial statements are due to be filed with the group's domiciliary regulator, make available to the commissioner an annual certification of each underwriter member's solvency by the member's domiciliary regulator and financial statements of each underwriter member of the group prepared by its independent public accountant.

Drafting Note: Unless otherwise stated, "commissioner" refers to the commissioner of insurance in the state where credit or a reduction from liability is taken.

Drafting Note: Consideration was given to deferring to state capital and surplus requirements as a threshold for the trusteed surplus, but it was concluded that, on the basis of risk exposure and current industry security practices, the standards for credit should be higher under Subsection D. The $100,000,000 trusteed surplus requirement for a group including incorporated and individual unincorporated underwriters reflects the higher financial standards currently found among the states for a group of this type. The $20,000,000 trusteed surplus requirement is an option available to assuming insurers that do not satisfy both the licensing and financial standards of Subsection B or C.

E. Credit shall be allowed when the reinsurance is ceded to an assuming insurer that has been certified by the commissioner as a reinsurer in this state and secures its obligations in accordance with the requirements of this subsection.

1. In order to be eligible for certification, the assuming insurer shall meet the following requirements:

    (a) The assuming insurer must be domiciled and licensed to transact insurance or reinsurance in a qualified jurisdiction, as determined by the commissioner pursuant to paragraph (3) of this subsection;
    (b) The assuming insurer must maintain minimum capital and surplus, or its equivalent, in an amount to be determined by the commissioner pursuant to regulation;
    (c) The assuming insurer must maintain financial strength ratings from two or more rating agencies deemed acceptable by the commissioner pursuant to regulation;
    (d) The assuming insurer must agree to submit to the jurisdiction of this state, appoint the commissioner as its agent for service of process in this state, and agree to provide security for 100 percent of the assuming insurer's liabilities attributable to reinsurance ceded by U.S. ceding insurers if it resists enforcement of a final U.S. judgment;
    (e) The assuming insurer must agree to meet applicable information filing requirements as determined by the

commissioner, both with respect to an initial application for certification and on an ongoing basis; and

(f) The assuming insurer must satisfy any other requirements for certification deemed relevant by the commissioner.

2. An association including incorporated and individual unincorporated underwriters may be a certified reinsurer. In order to be eligible for certification, in addition to satisfying requirements of paragraph (1):

   (a) The association shall satisfy its minimum capital and surplus requirements through the capital and surplus equivalents (net of liabilities) of the association and its members, which shall include a joint central fund that may be applied to any unsatisfied obligation of the association or any of its members, in an amount determined by the commissioner to provide adequate protection;
   (b) The incorporated members of the association shall not be engaged in any business other than underwriting as a member of the association and shall be subject to the same level of regulation and solvency control by the association's domiciliary regulator as are the unincorporated members; and
   (c) Within ninety (90) days after its financial statements are due to be filed with the association's domiciliary regulator, the association shall provide to the commissioner an annual certification by the association's domiciliary regulator of the solvency of each underwriter member; or if a certification is unavailable, financial statements, prepared by independent public accountants, of each underwriter member of the association.

3. The commissioner shall create and publish a list of qualified jurisdictions, under which an assuming insurer licensed and domiciled in such jurisdiction is eligible to be considered for certification by the commissioner as a certified reinsurer.

   (a) In order to determine whether the domiciliary jurisdiction of a non-U.S. assuming insurer is eligible to be recognized as a qualified jurisdiction, the commissioner shall evaluate the appropriateness and effectiveness of the reinsurance supervisory system of the jurisdiction, both initially and on an ongoing basis, and consider the rights, benefits and the extent of reciprocal recognition afforded by the non-U.S. jurisdiction to reinsurers licensed and domiciled in the U.S. A qualified jurisdiction must agree to share information and cooperate with the commissioner with respect to all certified reinsurers domiciled within that jurisdiction. A jurisdiction may not be recognized as a qualified jurisdiction if the commissioner has determined that the jurisdiction does not adequately and promptly enforce final U.S. judgments and arbitration awards. Additional factors may be considered in the discretion of the commissioner.

(b) A list of qualified jurisdictions shall be published through the NAIC Committee Process. The commissioner shall consider this list in determining qualified jurisdictions. If the commissioner approves a jurisdiction as qualified that does not appear on the list of qualified jurisdictions, the commissioner shall provide thoroughly documented justification in accordance with criteria to be developed under regulations.

(c) U.S. jurisdictions that meet the requirement for accreditation under the NAIC financial standards and accreditation program shall be recognized as qualified jurisdictions.

(d) If a certified reinsurer's domiciliary jurisdiction ceases to be a qualified jurisdiction, the commissioner has the discretion to suspend the reinsurer's certification indefinitely, in lieu of revocation.

4. The commissioner shall assign a rating to each certified reinsurer, giving due consideration to the financial strength ratings that have been assigned by rating agencies deemed acceptable to the commissioner pursuant to regulation. The commissioner shall publish a list of all certified reinsurers and their ratings.
5. A certified reinsurer shall secure obligations assumed from U.S. ceding insurers under this subsection at a level consistent with its rating, as specified in regulations promulgated by the commissioner.

(a) In order for a domestic ceding insurer to qualify for full financial statement credit for reinsurance ceded to a certified reinsurer, the certified reinsurer shall maintain security in a form acceptable to the commissioner and consistent with the provisions of Section 3, or in a multibeneficiary trust in accordance with Subsection D of this section, except as otherwise provided in this subsection.

(b) If a certified reinsurer maintains a trust to fully secure its obligations subject to Subsection D of this section, and chooses to secure its obligations incurred as a certified reinsurer in the form of a multibeneficiary trust, the certified reinsurer shall maintain separate trust accounts for its obligations incurred under reinsurance agreements issued or renewed as a certified reinsurer with reduced security as permitted by this subsection or comparable laws of other U.S. jurisdictions and for its obligations subject to Subsection D of this section. It shall be a condition to the grant of certification under Subsection E of this section that the certified reinsurer shall have bound itself, by the language of the trust and agreement with the commissioner with principal regulatory oversight of each such trust account, to fund, upon termination of any such trust account, out of the remaining surplus of such trust any deficiency of any other such trust account.

(c) The minimum trusteed surplus requirements provided in Subsection D are not applicable with respect to a multibeneficiary trust maintained by a certified reinsurer for the purpose of securing obligations incurred under this subsection, except that such trust shall maintain a minimum trusteed surplus of $10,000,000.

(d) With respect to obligations incurred by a certified reinsurer under this subsection, if the security is insufficient, the commissioner shall reduce the allowable credit by an amount proportionate to the deficiency, and has the discretion to impose further reductions in allowable credit upon finding that there is a material risk that the certified reinsurer's obligations will not be paid in full when due.

(e) For purposes of this subsection, a certified reinsurer whose certification has been terminated for any reason shall be treated as a certified reinsurer required to secure 100 percent of its obligations.

i. As used in this subsection, the term "terminated" refers to revocation, suspension, voluntary surrender and inactive status.
ii. If the commissioner continues to assign a higher rating as permitted by other provisions of this section, this requirement does not apply to a certified reinsurer in inactive status or to a reinsurer whose certification has been suspended.

6. If an applicant for certification has been certified as a reinsurer in an NAIC accredited jurisdiction, the commissioner has the discretion to defer to that jurisdiction's certification, and has the discretion to defer to the rating assigned by that jurisdiction, and such assuming insurer shall be considered to be a certified reinsurer in this state.
7. A certified reinsurer that ceases to assume new business in this state may request to maintain its certification in inactive status in order to continue to qualify for a reduction in security for its in-force business. An inactive certified reinsurer shall continue to comply with all applicable requirements of this subsection, and the commissioner shall assign a rating that takes into account, if relevant, the reasons why the reinsurer is not assuming new business.

F. Credit shall be allowed when the reinsurance is ceded to an assuming insurer not meeting the requirements of Subsections A, B, C, D or E of this section, but only as to the insurance of risks located in jurisdictions where the reinsurance is required by applicable law or regulation of that jurisdiction.

Drafting Note: For purposes of this subsection, "jurisdiction" refers to those jurisdictions other than the United States and also to any state, district or territory of the United States. Subsection E allows credit to ceding insurers that are mandated by these jurisdictions to cede to state-owned or controlled insurance or reinsurance companies or to participate in pools, guaranty associations or residual market mechanisms.

G. If the assuming insurer is not licensed, accredited or certified to transact insurance or reinsurance in this state, the credit permitted by Subsections C and D of this section shall not be allowed unless the assuming insurer agrees in the reinsurance agreements:

1.

(a) That in the event of the failure of the assuming insurer to perform its obligations under the terms of the reinsurance agreement, the assuming insurer, at the request of the ceding insurer, shall submit to the jurisdiction of any court of competent jurisdiction in any state of the United States, will comply with all requirements necessary to give the court jurisdiction, and will abide by the final decision of the court or of any appellate court in the event of an appeal; and

(b) To designate the commissioner or a designated attorney as its true and lawful attorney upon whom may be served any lawful process in any action, suit or proceeding instituted by or on behalf of the ceding insurer.

2. This subsection is not intended to conflict with or override the obligation of the parties to a reinsurance agreement to arbitrate their disputes, if this obligation is created in the agreement.

H. If the assuming insurer does not meet the requirements of Subsections A, B or C, the credit permitted by Subsection D or E of this section shall not be allowed unless the assuming insurer agrees in the trust agreements to the following conditions:

1. Notwithstanding any other provisions in the trust instrument, if the trust fund is inadequate because it contains an amount less than the amount required by Subsection D(3) of this section, or if the

grantor of the trust has been declared insolvent or placed into receivership, rehabilitation, liquidation or similar proceedings under the laws of its state or country of domicile, the trustee shall comply with an order of the commissioner with regulatory oversight over the trust or with an order of a court of competent jurisdiction directing the trustee to transfer to the commissioner with regulatory oversight all of the assets of the trust fund.

2. The assets shall be distributed by and claims shall be filed with and valued by the commissioner with regulatory oversight in accordance with the laws of the state in which the trust is domiciled that are applicable to the liquidation of domestic insurance companies.
3. If the commissioner with regulatory oversight determines that the assets of the trust fund or any part thereof are not necessary to satisfy the claims of the U.S. ceding insurers of the grantor of the trust, the assets or part thereof shall be returned by the commissioner with regulatory oversight to the trustee for distribution in accordance with the trust agreement.
4. The grantor shall waive any right otherwise available to it under U.S. law that is inconsistent with this provision.

I. If an accredited or certified reinsurer ceases to meet the requirements for accreditation or certification, the commissioner may suspend or revoke the reinsurer's accreditation or certification.

1. The commissioner must give the reinsurer notice and opportunity for hearing. The suspension or revocation may not take effect until after the commissioner's order on hearing, unless:

(a) The reinsurer waives its right to hearing;
(b) The commissioner's order is based on regulatory action by the reinsurer's domiciliary jurisdiction or the voluntary surrender or termination of the reinsurer's eligibility to transact insurance or reinsurance business in its domiciliary jurisdiction or in the primary certifying state of the reinsurer under Subparagraph E(6) of this section; or
(c) The commissioner finds that an emergency requires immediate action and a court of competent jurisdiction has not stayed the commissioner's action.

2. While a reinsurer's accreditation or certification is suspended, no reinsurance contract issued or renewed after the effective date of the suspension qualifies for credit except to the extent that the reinsurer's obligations under the contract are secured in accordance with Section 3. If a reinsurer's accreditation or certification is revoked, no credit for reinsurance may be granted after the effective date of the revocation except to the extent that the reinsurer's obligations under the contract are secured in accordance with Subsection E(5) or Section 3.

J. Concentration Risk.

1. A ceding insurer shall take steps to manage its reinsurance recoverables proportionate to its own book of business. A domestic ceding insurer shall notify the commissioner within thirty (30) days after reinsurance recoverables from any single assuming insurer, or group of affiliated assuming insurers, exceeds fifty percent (50%) of the domestic ceding insurer's last reported surplus to policyholders, or after it is determined that reinsurance recoverables from any single assuming insurer, or group of affiliated assuming insurers, is likely to exceed this limit. The notification shall demonstrate that the exposure is safely managed by the domestic ceding insurer.
2. A ceding insurer shall take steps to diversify its reinsurance program. A domestic ceding insurer shall notify the commissioner within thirty (30) days after ceding to any single assuming insurer, or group of affiliated assuming insurers, more than twenty percent (20%) of the ceding insurer's gross written premium in the prior calendar year, or after it has determined that the reinsurance ceded to any single assuming insurer, or group of affiliated assuming insurers, is likely to exceed this limit. The notification shall demonstrate that the exposure is safely managed by the domestic ceding insurer.

Courtesy of Leah Campbell and Donald B. Henderson Jr., Wilkie Farr & Gallagher LLP

APPENDIX B

MODEL 786 S 8

Credit for Reinsurance—Certified Reinsurers

A. Pursuant to [cite state law equivalent of Section 2E of the Credit for Reinsurance Model Law], the commissioner shall allow credit for reinsurance ceded by a domestic insurer to an assuming insurer that has been certified as a reinsurer in this state at all times for which statutory financial statement credit for reinsurance is claimed under this section. The credit allowed shall be based upon the security held by or on behalf of the ceding insurer in accordance with a rating assigned to the certified reinsurer by the commissioner. The security shall be in a form consistent with the provisions of [cite state law equivalent of Section 2E and Section 3 of the Credit for Reinsurance Model Law] and 11, 12 or 13 of this Regulation. The amount of security required in order for full credit to be allowed shall correspond with the following requirements:

1.

Ratings	Security Required
Secure – 1	0%
Secure – 2	10%
Secure – 3	20%
Secure – 4	50%
Secure – 5	75%
Vulnerable – 6	100%

2. Affiliated reinsurance transactions shall receive the same opportunity for reduced security requirements as all other reinsurance transactions.
3. The commissioner shall require the certified reinsurer to post one hundred percent (100%), for the benefit of the ceding insurer or its estate, security upon the entry of an order of rehabilitation, liquidation or conservation against the ceding insurer.

4. In order to facilitate the prompt payment of claims, a certified reinsurer shall not be required to post security for catastrophe recoverables for a period of one year from the date of the first instance of a liability reserve entry by the ceding company as a result of a loss from a catastrophic occurrence as recognized by the commissioner. The one year deferral period is contingent upon the certified reinsurer continuing to pay claims in a timely manner. Reinsurance recoverables for only the following lines of business as reported on the NAIC annual financial statement related specifically to the catastrophic occurrence will be included in the deferral:

   (a) Line 1: Fire
   (b) Line 2: Allied Lines
   (c) Line 3: Farmowners multiple peril
   (d) Line 4: Homeowners multiple peril
   (e) Line 5: Commercial multiple peril
   (f) Line 9: Inland Marine
   (g) Line 12: Earthquake
   (h) Line 21: Auto physical damage

5. Credit for reinsurance under this section shall apply only to reinsurance contracts entered into or renewed on or after the effective date of the certification of the assuming insurer. Any reinsurance contract entered into prior to the effective date of the certification of the assuming insurer that is subsequently amended after the effective date of the certification of the assuming insurer, or a new reinsurance contract, covering any risk for which collateral was provided previously, shall only be subject to this section with respect to losses incurred and reserves reported from and after the effective date of the amendment or new contract.
6. Nothing in this section shall prohibit the parties to a reinsurance agreement from agreeing to provisions establishing security requirements that exceed the minimum security requirements established for certified reinsurers under this section.

B. Certification Procedure.

1. The commissioner shall post notice on the insurance department's website promptly upon receipt of any application for certification, including instructions on how members of the public may respond to the application. The commissioner may not take final action on the application until at least thirty (30) days after posting the notice required by this paragraph.

Drafting Note: States that do not wish to make the internet the required mechanism for providing public notice should modify this provision accordingly. This provision was intended to provide a less formal notice requirement than is typically called for under state Administrative Procedure Acts.

2. The commissioner shall issue written notice to an assuming insurer that has made application and been approved as a certified reinsurer. Included in such notice shall be the rating assigned the certified reinsurer in accordance with Subsection A of this section. The commissioner shall publish a list of all certified reinsurers and their ratings.
3. In order to be eligible for certification, the assuming insurer shall meet the following requirements:

   (a) The assuming insurer must be domiciled and licensed to transact insurance or reinsurance in a Qualified Jurisdiction, as determined by the commissioner pursuant to Subsection C of this section.
   (b) The assuming insurer must maintain capital and surplus, or its equivalent, of no less than $250,000,000 calculated in accordance with Subparagraph (4)(h) of this subsection. This requirement may also be satisfied by an association including incorporated and individual unincorporated underwriters having minimum capital and surplus equivalents (net of liabilities) of at least $250,000,000 and a central fund containing a balance of at least $250,000,000.
   (c) The assuming insurer must maintain financial strength ratings from two or more rating agencies deemed

acceptable by the commissioner. These ratings shall be based on interactive communication between the rating agency and the assuming insurer and shall not be based solely on publicly available information. These financial strength ratings will be one factor used by the commissioner in determining the rating that is assigned to the assuming insurer. Acceptable rating agencies include the following:

i. Standard & Poor's;
ii. Moody's Investors Service;
iii. Fitch Ratings;
iv. A.M. Best Company; or
v. Any other Nationally Recognized Statistical Rating Organization.

(d) The certified reinsurer must comply with any other requirements reasonably imposed by the commissioner.

4. Each certified reinsurer shall be rated on a legal entity basis, with due consideration being given to the group rating where appropriate, except that an association including incorporated and individual unincorporated underwriters that has been approved to do business as a single certified reinsurer may be evaluated on the basis of its group rating. Factors that may be considered as part of the evaluation process include, but are not limited to, the following:

(a) The certified reinsurer's financial strength rating from an acceptable rating agency. The maximum rating that a certified reinsurer may be assigned will correspond to its financial strength rating as outlined in the table below. The commissioner shall use the lowest financial strength rating received from an approved rating agency in establishing the maximum rating of a certified reinsurer. A failure to obtain or maintain at least two financial strength ratings from acceptable rating agencies will result in loss of eligibility for certification:

Ratings	Best	S&P	Moody's	Fitch
Secure – 1	A++	AAA	Aaa	AAA
Secure – 2	A+	AA+, AA, AA-	Aa1, Aa2, Aa3	AA+, AA, AA-
Secure – 3	A	A+, A	A1, A2	A+, A
Secure – 4	A-	A-	A3	A-
Secure – 5	B++, B+	BBB+, BBB, BBB-	Baa1, Baa2, Baa3	BBB+, BBB, BBB-
Vulnerable – 6	B, B- C++, C+, C, C-, D, E, F	BB+, BB, BB-, B+, B, B-, CCC, CC, C, D, R	Ba1, Ba2, Ba3, B1, B2, B3, Caa, Ca, C	BB+, BB, BB-, B+, B, B-, CCC+, CC, CCC-, DD

(b) The business practices of the certified reinsurer in dealing with its ceding insurers, including its record of compliance with reinsurance contractual terms and obligations;

(c) For certified reinsurers domiciled in the U.S., a review of the most recent applicable NAIC Annual Statement Blank, either Schedule F (for property/casualty reinsurers) or Schedule S (for life and health reinsurers);

(d) For certified reinsurers not domiciled in the U.S., a review annually of Form CR-F (for property/casualty reinsurers) or Form CR-S (for life and health reinsurers) (attached as exhibits to this regulation);

(e) The reputation of the certified reinsurer for prompt payment of claims under reinsurance agreements, based on an analysis of ceding insurers' Schedule F reporting of overdue reinsurance recoverables, including the proportion of obligations that are more than ninety (90) days past due or are in dispute, with specific attention given to obligations payable to companies that are in administrative supervision or receivership;

(f) Regulatory actions against the certified reinsurer;

(g) The report of the independent auditor on the financial statements of the insurance enterprise, on the basis described in paragraph (h) below;

(h) For certified reinsurers not domiciled in the U.S., audited financial statements (audited U.S. GAAP basis if available, audited IFRS basis statements are allowed but must include an audited footnote reconciling equity and net income to a U.S. GAAP basis, or, with the permission of the state insurance commissioner, audited IFRS statements with reconciliation to U.S. GAAP certified by an officer of the company), regulatory filings, and actuarial opinion (as filed with the non-U.S. jurisdiction supervisor). Upon the initial application for certification, the commissioner will consider audited financial statements for the last three (3) years filed with its non-U.S. jurisdiction supervisor;

(i) The liquidation priority of obligations to a ceding insurer in the certified reinsurer's domiciliary jurisdiction in the context of an insolvency proceeding;

(j) A certified reinsurer's participation in any solvent scheme of arrangement, or similar procedure, which involves U.S. ceding insurers. The commissioner shall receive prior notice from a certified reinsurer that proposes participation by the certified reinsurer in a solvent scheme of arrangement; and

(k) Any other information deemed relevant by the commissioner.

5. Based on the analysis conducted under Subparagraph (4)(e) of a certified reinsurer's reputation for prompt payment of claims, the commissioner may make appropriate adjustments in the security the certified reinsurer is required to post to protect its liabilities to U.S. ceding insurers, provided that the commissioner shall, at a minimum, increase the security the certified reinsurer is required to post by one rating level under Subparagraph (4)(a) if the commissioner finds that:

(a) more than fifteen percent (15%) of the certified reinsurer's ceding insurance clients have overdue reinsurance recoverables on paid losses of ninety (90) days or more which are not in dispute and which exceed $100,000 for each cedent; or

(b) the aggregate amount of reinsurance recoverables on paid losses which are not in dispute that are overdue by ninety (90) days or more exceeds $50,000,000.

6. The assuming insurer must submit a properly executed Form CR-1 (attached as an exhibit to this regulation) as evidence of its submission to the jurisdiction of this state, appointment of the commissioner as an agent for service of process in this state, and agreement to provide security for one hundred percent (100%) of the assuming insurer's liabilities attributable to reinsurance ceded by U.S. ceding insurers if it resists enforcement of a final U.S. judgment. The commissioner shall not certify any assuming insurer that is domiciled in a jurisdiction that the commissioner has determined does not adequately and promptly enforce final U.S. judgments or arbitration awards.
7. The certified reinsurer must agree to meet applicable information filing requirements as determined by the commissioner, both with respect to an initial application for certification and on an ongoing basis. All information submitted by certified reinsurers which are not otherwise public information subject to disclosure shall be exempted from disclosure under [cite state law equivalent of Freedom of Information Act] and shall be withheld from public disclosure. The applicable information filing requirements are, as follows:

    (a) Notification within ten (10) days of any regulatory actions taken against the certified reinsurer, any change in the provisions of its domiciliary license or any change in rating by an approved rating agency, including a statement describing such changes and the reasons therefore;
    (b) Annually, Form CR-F or CR-S, as applicable [per the instructions to be developed as an exhibit to this model];
    (c) Annually, the report of the independent auditor on the financial statements of the insurance enterprise, on the basis described in Subsection (d) below;
    (d) Annually, audited financial statements (audited U.S. GAAP basis if available, audited IFRS basis statements are allowed but must include an audited footnote reconciling equity and net income to a U.S. GAAP basis, or, with the permission of the state insurance commissioner, audited IFRS statements with reconciliation to U.S. GAAP certified by an officer of

the company), regulatory filings, and actuarial opinion (as filed with the certified reinsurer's supervisor). Upon the initial certification, audited financial statements for the last three (3) years filed with the certified reinsurer's supervisor;

(e) At least annually, an updated list of all disputed and overdue reinsurance claims regarding reinsurance assumed from U.S. domestic ceding insurers;

(f) A certification from the certified reinsurer's domestic regulator that the certified reinsurer is in good standing and maintains capital in excess of the jurisdiction's highest regulatory action level; and

(g) Any other information that the commissioner may reasonably require.

8. Change in Rating or Revocation of Certification.

(a) In the case of a downgrade by a rating agency or other disqualifying circumstance, the commissioner shall upon written notice assign a new rating to the certified reinsurer in accordance with the requirements of Subparagraph (4)(a).

(b) The commissioner shall have the authority to suspend, revoke, or otherwise modify a certified reinsurer's certification at any time if the certified reinsurer fails to meet its obligations or security requirements under this section, or if other financial or operating results of the certified reinsurer, or documented significant delays in payment by the certified reinsurer, lead the commissioner to reconsider the certified reinsurer's ability or willingness to meet its contractual obligations.

(c) If the rating of a certified reinsurer is upgraded by the commissioner, the certified reinsurer may meet the security requirements applicable to its new rating on a prospective basis, but the commissioner shall require the certified reinsurer to post security under the previously applicable security requirements as to all contracts in force on or before the effective date of the upgraded rating. If the rating of a certified reinsurer is downgraded by the commissioner, the commissioner shall require the certified reinsurer to meet the security requirements applicable to its new rating for all business it has assumed as a certified reinsurer.

(d) Upon revocation of the certification of a certified reinsurer by the commissioner, the assuming insurer shall be required to post security in accordance with Section 10 in order for the ceding insurer to continue to take credit for reinsurance ceded to the assuming insurer. If funds continue to be held in trust in accordance with Section 7, the commissioner may allow additional credit equal to the ceding insurer's pro rata share of such funds, discounted to reflect the risk of uncollectibility and anticipated expenses of trust administration. Notwithstanding the change of a certified reinsurer's rating or revocation of its certification, a domestic insurer that has ceded reinsurance to that certified reinsurer may not be denied credit for reinsurance for a period of three (3) months for all reinsurance ceded to that certified reinsurer, unless the reinsurance is found by the commissioner to be at high risk of uncollectibility.

C. Qualified Jurisdictions.

1. If, upon conducting an evaluation under this section with respect to the reinsurance supervisory system of any non-U.S. assuming insurer, the commissioner determines that the jurisdiction qualifies to be recognized as a qualified jurisdiction, the commissioner shall publish notice and evidence of such recognition in an appropriate manner. The commissioner may establish a procedure to withdraw recognition of those jurisdictions that are no longer qualified.
2. In order to determine whether the domiciliary jurisdiction of a non-U.S. assuming insurer is eligible to be recognized as a qualified jurisdiction, the commissioner shall evaluate the reinsurance supervisory system of the non-U.S. jurisdiction, both initially and on an ongoing basis, and consider the rights, benefits and the extent of reciprocal recognition afforded by the non-U.S. jurisdiction to reinsurers licensed and domiciled in the U.S. The commissioner shall determine the appropriate approach for evaluating the qualifications of such jurisdictions,

and create and publish a list of jurisdictions whose reinsurers may be approved by the commissioner as eligible for certification. A qualified jurisdiction must agree to share information and cooperate with the commissioner with respect to all certified reinsurers domiciled within that jurisdiction. Additional factors to be considered in determining whether to recognize a qualified jurisdiction, in the discretion of the commissioner, include but are not limited to the following:

(a) The framework under which the assuming insurer is regulated.
(b) The structure and authority of the domiciliary regulator with regard to solvency regulation requirements and financial surveillance.
(c) The substance of financial and operating standards for assuming insurers in the domiciliary jurisdiction.
(d) The form and substance of financial reports required to be filed or made publicly available by reinsurers in the domiciliary jurisdiction and the accounting principles used.
(e) The domiciliary regulator's willingness to cooperate with U.S. regulators in general and the commissioner in particular.
(f) The history of performance by assuming insurers in the domiciliary jurisdiction.
(g) Any documented evidence of substantial problems with the enforcement of final U.S. judgments in the domiciliary jurisdiction. A jurisdiction will not be considered to be a qualified jurisdiction if the commissioner has determined that it does not adequately and promptly enforce final U.S. judgments or arbitration awards.
(h) Any relevant international standards or guidance with respect to mutual recognition of reinsurance supervision adopted by the International Association of Insurance Supervisors or successor organization.
(i) Any other matters deemed relevant by the commissioner.

3. A list of qualified jurisdictions shall be published through the NAIC Committee Process. The commissioner shall consider this list in determining qualified jurisdictions. If the commissioner approves a jurisdiction as qualified that does not

appear on the list of qualified jurisdictions, the commissioner shall provide thoroughly documented justification with respect to the criteria provided under Subsections 8.C(2)(a) to (i).

4. U.S. jurisdictions that meet the requirements for accreditation under the NAIC financial standards and accreditation program shall be recognized as qualified jurisdictions.

D. Recognition of Certification Issued by an NAIC Accredited Jurisdiction.

1. If an applicant for certification has been certified as a reinsurer in an NAIC accredited jurisdiction, the commissioner has the discretion to defer to that jurisdiction's certification, and to defer to the rating assigned by that jurisdiction, if the assuming insurer submits a properly executed Form CR-1 and such additional information as the commissioner requires. The assuming insurer shall be considered to be a certified reinsurer in this State.
2. Any change in the certified reinsurer's status or rating in the other jurisdiction shall apply automatically in this State as of the date it takes effect in the other jurisdiction. The certified reinsurer shall notify the commissioner of any change in its status or rating within 10 days after receiving notice of the change.
3. The commissioner may withdraw recognition of the other jurisdiction's rating at any time and assign a new rating in accordance with Subsection B(8) of this section.
4. The commissioner may withdraw recognition of the other jurisdiction's certification at any time, with written notice to the certified reinsurer. Unless the commissioner suspends or revokes the certified reinsurer's certification in accordance with Subsection B(8) of this section, the certified reinsurer's certification shall remain in good standing in this State for a period of three (3) months, which shall be extended if additional time is necessary to consider the assuming insurer's application for certification in this State.

E. Mandatory Funding Clause. In addition to the clauses required under Section 14, reinsurance contracts entered into or renewed under this section shall include a proper funding clause, which requires the certified reinsurer to provide and maintain security in an amount sufficient to avoid the imposition of any financial statement penalty on the ceding insurer under this section for reinsurance ceded to the certified reinsurer.

F. The commissioner shall comply with all reporting and notification requirements that may be established by the NAIC with respect to certified reinsurers and qualified jurisdictions.

Courtesy of Leah Campbell and Donald B. Henderson Jr., Wilkie Farr & Gallagher LLP

APPENDIX C

MODEL 786 S 10

Asset or Reduction from Liability for Reinsurance Ceded to an Unauthorized Assuming Insurer Not Meeting the Requirements of Sections 4 Through 9

A. Pursuant to Section [cite state law equivalent of Section 3 of the Credit for Reinsurance Model Law], the commissioner shall allow a reduction from liability for reinsurance ceded by a domestic insurer to an assuming insurer not meeting the requirements of Section [cite state law equivalent of Section 2 or other appropriate section of the Credit for Reinsurance Model Law] in an amount not exceeding the liabilities carried by the ceding insurer. The reduction shall be in the amount of funds held by or on behalf of the ceding insurer, including funds held in trust for the exclusive benefit of the ceding insurer, under a reinsurance contract with such assuming insurer as security for the payment of obligations under the reinsurance contract. The security shall be held in the United States subject to withdrawal solely by, and under the exclusive control of, the ceding insurer or, in the case of a trust, held in a qualified United States financial institution as defined in Section [cite state law equivalent of Section 4B of the Credit for Reinsurance Model Law]. This security may be in the form of any of the following:

1. Cash;
2. Securities listed by the Securities Valuation Office of the NAIC, including those deemed exempt from filing as defined by the Purposes and Procedures Manual of the Securities Valuation Office, and qualifying as admitted assets;
3. Clean, irrevocable, unconditional and "evergreen" letters of credit issued or confirmed by a qualified United States institution, as defined in Section [cite state law equivalent of Section 4A of the Credit for Reinsurance Model Law], effective no later than December 31 of the year for which filing is being made, and in the possession of, or in trust for, the ceding insurer on or before the filing date of its annual statement.

Letters of credit meeting applicable standards of issuer acceptability as of the dates of their issuance (or confirmation) shall, notwithstanding the issuing (or confirming) institution's subsequent failure to meet applicable standards of issuer acceptability, continue to be acceptable as security until their expiration, extension, renewal, modification or amendment, whichever first occurs; or

4. Any other form of security acceptable to the commissioner.
5. An admitted asset or a reduction from liability for reinsurance ceded to an unauthorized assuming insurer pursuant to this section shall be allowed only when the requirements of Section 14 and the applicable portions of Sections 11, 12 or 13 of this regulation have been satisfied.

Courtesy of Leah Campbell and Donald B. Henderson Jr., Wilkie Farr & Gallagher LLP

APPENDIX D

MODEL 786 S 11

Trust Agreements Qualified Under Section 10

A. As used in this section:

1. "Beneficiary" means the entity for whose sole benefit the trust has been established and any successor of the beneficiary by operation of law. If a court of law appoints a successor in interest to the named beneficiary, then the named beneficiary includes and is limited to the court appointed domiciliary receiver (including conservator, rehabilitator or liquidator).

Drafting Note: The NAIC has adopted the above definition as part of the "Uniform Letter of Credit." However, the state may choose to utilize the following definition: "Beneficiary" includes any successor by operation of law of the named beneficiary, including without limitation any liquidator, rehabilitator, receiver or conservator.

2. "Grantor" means the entity that has established a trust for the sole benefit of the beneficiary. When established in conjunction with a reinsurance agreement, the grantor is the unlicensed, unaccredited assuming insurer.
3. "Obligations," as used Subsection B(11) of this section means:

(a) Reinsured losses and allocated loss expenses paid by the ceding company, but not recovered from the assuming insurer;
(b) Reserves for reinsured losses reported and outstanding;
(c) Reserves for reinsured losses incurred but not reported; and
(d) Reserves for allocated reinsured loss expenses and unearned premiums.

B. Required conditions.

1. The trust agreement shall be entered into between the beneficiary, the grantor and a trustee, which shall be a qualified

United States financial institution as defined in Section [insert citation to state law equivalent to Section 4B of the Credit for Reinsurance Model Law].

2. The trust agreement shall create a trust account into which assets shall be deposited.
3. All assets in the trust account shall be held by the trustee at the trustee's office in the United States.
4. The trust agreement shall provide that:

   (a) The beneficiary shall have the right to withdraw assets from the trust account at any time, without notice to the grantor, subject only to written notice from the beneficiary to the trustee;
   (b) No other statement or document is required to be presented to withdraw assets, except that the beneficiary may be required to acknowledge receipt of withdrawn assets;
   (c) It is not subject to any conditions or qualifications outside of the trust agreement; and
   (d) It shall not contain references to any other agreements or documents except as provided for in Paragraphs (11) and (12) of this subsection.

5. The trust agreement shall be established for the sole benefit of the beneficiary.
6. The trust agreement shall require the trustee to:

   (a) Receive assets and hold all assets in a safe place;
   (b) Determine that all assets are in such form that the beneficiary, or the trustee upon direction by the beneficiary, may whenever necessary negotiate any such assets, without consent or signature from the grantor or any other person or entity;
   (c) Furnish to the grantor and the beneficiary a statement of all assets in the trust account upon its inception and at intervals no less frequent than the end of each calendar quarter;
   (d) Notify the grantor and the beneficiary within ten (10) days, of any deposits to or withdrawals from the trust account;

(e) Upon written demand of the beneficiary, immediately take any and all steps necessary to transfer absolutely and unequivocally all right, title and interest in the assets held in the trust account to the beneficiary and deliver physical custody of the assets to the beneficiary; and

(f) Allow no substitutions or withdrawals of assets from the trust account, except on written instructions from the beneficiary, except that the trustee may, without the consent of but with notice to the beneficiary, upon call or maturity of any trust asset, withdraw such asset upon condition that the proceeds are paid into the trust account.

7. The trust agreement shall provide that at least thirty (30) days, but not more than forty-five (45) days, prior to termination of the trust account, written notification of termination shall be delivered by the trustee to the beneficiary.
8. The trust agreement shall be made subject to and governed by the laws of the state in which the trust is domiciled.
9. The trust agreement shall prohibit invasion of the trust corpus for the purpose of paying commission to, or reimbursing the expenses of, the trustee. In order for a letter of credit to qualify as an asset of the trust, the trustee shall have the right and the obligation pursuant to the deed of trust or some other binding agreement (as duly approved by the commissioner), to immediately draw down the full amount of the letter of credit and hold the proceeds in trust for the beneficiaries of the trust if the letter of credit will otherwise expire without being renewed or replaced.
10. The trust agreement shall provide that the trustee shall be liable for its negligence, willful misconduct or lack of good faith. The failure of the trustee to draw against the letter of credit in circumstances where such draw would be required shall be deemed to be negligence and/or willful misconduct.
11. Notwithstanding other provisions of this regulation, when a trust agreement is established in conjunction with a reinsurance agreement covering risks other than life, annuities and accident and health, where it is customary practice to provide a trust agreement for a specific purpose, the trust agreement may provide that the ceding insurer shall undertake to use and apply

amounts drawn upon the trust account, without diminution because of the insolvency of the ceding insurer or the assuming insurer, only for the following purposes:

(a) To pay or reimburse the ceding insurer for the assuming insurer's share under the specific reinsurance agreement regarding any losses and allocated loss expenses paid by the ceding insurer, but not recovered from the assuming insurer, or for unearned premiums due to the ceding insurer if not otherwise paid by the assuming insurer;

(b) To make payment to the assuming insurer of any amounts held in the trust account that exceed 102 percent of the actual amount required to fund the assuming insurer's obligations under the specific reinsurance agreement; or

(c) Where the ceding insurer has received notification of termination of the trust account and where the assuming insurer's entire obligations under the specific reinsurance agreement remain unliquidated and undischarged ten (10) days prior to the termination date, to withdraw amounts equal to the obligations and deposit those amounts in a separate account, in the name of the ceding insurer in any qualified U.S. financial institution as defined in Section [insert citation to state law equivalent of Section 4B of the Credit for Reinsurance Model Law] apart from its general assets, in trust for such uses and purposes specified in Subparagraphs (a) and (b) above as may remain executory after such withdrawal and for any period after the termination date.

12. Notwithstanding other provisions of this regulation, when a trust agreement is established to meet the requirements of Section 10 in conjunction with a reinsurance agreement covering life, annuities or accident and health risks, where it is customary to provide a trust agreement for a specific purpose, the trust agreement may provide that the ceding insurer shall undertake to use and apply amounts drawn upon the trust account, without diminution because of the insolvency of the ceding insurer or the assuming insurer, only for the following purposes:

(a) To pay or reimburse the ceding insurer for:

   i. The assuming insurer's share under the specific reinsurance agreement of premiums returned, but not yet recovered from the assuming insurer, to the owners of policies reinsured under the reinsurance agreement on account of cancellations of the policies; and
   ii. The assuming insurer's share under the specific reinsurance agreement of surrenders and benefits or losses paid by the ceding insurer, but not yet recovered from the assuming insurer, under the terms and provisions of the policies reinsured under the reinsurance agreement;

(b) To pay to the assuming insurer amounts held in the trust account in excess of the amount necessary to secure the credit or reduction from liability for reinsurance taken by the ceding insurer; or
(c) Where the ceding insurer has received notification of termination of the trust and where the assuming insurer's entire obligations under the specific reinsurance agreement remain unliquidated and undischarged ten (10) days prior to the termination date, to withdraw amounts equal to the assuming insurer's share of liabilities, to the extent that the liabilities have not yet been funded by the assuming insurer, and deposit those amounts in a separate account, in the name of the ceding insurer in any qualified U.S. financial institution apart from its general assets, in trust for the uses and purposes specified in Subparagraphs (a) and (b) of this paragraph as may remain executory after withdrawal and for any period after the termination date.

13. Either the reinsurance agreement or the trust agreement must stipulate that assets deposited in the trust account shall be valued according to their current fair market value and shall consist only of cash in United States dollars, certificates of deposit issued by a United States bank and payable in United States dollars, and investments permitted by the Insurance Code or any combination of the above, provided investments in or issued by an entity

controlling, controlled by or under common control with either the grantor or the beneficiary of the trust shall not exceed five percent (5%) of total investments. The agreement may further specify the types of investments to be deposited. If the reinsurance agreement covers life, annuities or accident and health risks, then the provisions required by this paragraph must be included in the reinsurance agreement.

C. Permitted conditions.

1. The trust agreement may provide that the trustee may resign upon delivery of a written notice of resignation, effective not less than ninety (90) days after the beneficiary and grantor receive the notice and that the trustee may be removed by the grantor by delivery to the trustee and the beneficiary of a written notice of removal, effective not less than ninety (90) days after the trustee and the beneficiary receive the notice, provided that no such resignation or removal shall be effective until a successor trustee has been duly appointed and approved by the beneficiary and the grantor and all assets in the trust have been duly transferred to the new trustee.
2. The grantor may have the full and unqualified right to vote any shares of stock in the trust account and to receive from time to time payments of any dividends or interest upon any shares of stock or obligations included in the trust account. Any interest or dividends shall be either forwarded promptly upon receipt to the grantor or deposited in a separate account established in the grantor's name.
3. The trustee may be given authority to invest, and accept substitutions of, any funds in the account, provided that no investment or substitution shall be made without prior approval of the beneficiary, unless the trust agreement specifies categories of investments acceptable to the beneficiary and authorizes the trustee to invest funds and to accept substitutions that the trustee determines are at least equal in current fair market value to the assets withdrawn and that are consistent with the restrictions in Subsection D(1)(b) of this section.
4. The trust agreement may provide that the beneficiary may at any time designate a party to which all or part of the trust assets are to

be transferred. Transfer may be conditioned upon the trustee receiving, prior to or simultaneously, other specified assets.

5. The trust agreement may provide that, upon termination of the trust account, all assets not previously withdrawn by the beneficiary shall, with written approval by the beneficiary, be delivered over to the grantor.

D. Additional conditions applicable to reinsurance agreements:

A. A reinsurance agreement may contain provisions that:

(a) Require the assuming insurer to enter into a trust agreement and to establish a trust account for the benefit of the ceding insurer, and specifying what the agreement is to cover;
(b) Require the assuming insurer, prior to depositing assets with the trustee, to execute assignments or endorsements in blank, or to transfer legal title to the trustee of all shares, obligations or any other assets requiring assignments, in order that the ceding insurer, or the trustee upon the direction of the ceding insurer, may whenever necessary negotiate these assets without consent or signature from the assuming insurer or any other entity;
(c) Require that all settlements of account between the ceding insurer and the assuming insurer be made in cash or its equivalent; and
(d) Stipulate that the assuming insurer and the ceding insurer agree that the assets in the trust account, established pursuant to the provisions of the reinsurance agreement, may be withdrawn by the ceding insurer at any time, notwithstanding any other provisions in the reinsurance agreement, and shall be utilized and applied by the ceding insurer or its successors in interest by operation of law, including without limitation any liquidator, rehabilitator, receiver or conservator of such company, without diminution because of insolvency on the part of the ceding insurer or the assuming insurer, only for the following purposes:

i. To pay or reimburse the ceding insurer for:

(I) The assuming insurer's share under the specific reinsurance agreement of premiums returned, but not yet recovered from the assuming insurer, to the owners of policies reinsured under the reinsurance agreement because of cancellations of such policies;

(II) The assuming insurer's share of surrenders and benefits or losses paid by the ceding insurer pursuant to the provisions of the policies reinsured under the reinsurance agreement; and

(III) Any other amounts necessary to secure the credit or reduction from liability for reinsurance taken by the ceding insurer;

ii. To make payment to the assuming insurer of amounts held in the trust account in excess of the amount necessary to secure the credit or reduction from liability for reinsurance taken by the ceding insurer.

B. The reinsurance agreement also may contain provisions that:

(a) Give the assuming insurer the right to seek approval from the ceding insurer, which shall not be unreasonably or arbitrarily withheld, to withdraw from the trust account all or any part of the trust assets and transfer those assets to the assuming insurer, provided:

i. The assuming insurer shall, at the time of withdrawal, replace the withdrawn assets with other qualified assets having a current fair market value equal to the market value of the assets withdrawn so as to maintain at all times the deposit in the required amount; or

ii. After withdrawal and transfer, the current fair market value of the trust account is no less than 102 percent of the required amount.

(b) Provide for the return of any amount withdrawn in excess of the actual amounts required for Paragraph (1)(d) of this subsection, and for interest payments at a rate not in excess of the prime rate of interest on such amounts;

(c) Permit the award by any arbitration panel or court of competent jurisdiction of:

  i. Interest at a rate different from that provided in Subparagraph (b) of this paragraph;
  ii. Court or arbitration costs;
  iii. Attorney's fees; and
  iv. Any other reasonable expenses.

E. Financial reporting. A trust agreement may be used to reduce any liability for reinsurance ceded to an unauthorized assuming insurer in financial statements required to be filed with this department in compliance with the provisions of this regulation when established on or before the date of filing of the financial statement of the ceding insurer. Further, the reduction for the existence of an acceptable trust account may be up to the current fair market value of acceptable assets available to be withdrawn from the trust account at that time, but such reduction shall be no greater than the specific obligations under the reinsurance agreement that the trust account was established to secure.

F. Existing agreements. Notwithstanding the effective date of this regulation, any trust agreement or underlying reinsurance agreement in existence prior to [insert date] will continue to be acceptable until [insert date], at which time the agreements will have to fully comply with this regulation for the trust agreement to be acceptable.

G. The failure of any trust agreement to specifically identify the beneficiary as defined in Subsection A of this section shall not be construed to affect any actions or rights that the commissioner may take or possess pursuant to the provisions of the laws of this state.

Courtesy of Leah Campbell and Donald B. Henderson Jr., Wilkie Farr & Gallagher LLP

APPENDIX E

MODEL 786 S 12

Letters of Credit Qualified Under Section 10

A. The letter of credit must be clean, irrevocable, unconditional and issued or confirmed by a qualified United States financial institution as defined in Section [insert citation to state law equivalent of Section 4A of the Credit for Reinsurance Model Law]. The letter of credit shall contain an issue date and expiration date and shall stipulate that the beneficiary need only draw a sight draft under the letter of credit and present it to obtain funds and that no other document need be presented. The letter of credit also shall indicate that it is not subject to any condition or qualifications outside of the letter of credit. In addition, the letter of credit itself shall not contain reference to any other agreements, documents or entities, except as provided in Subsection I(1) of this section. As used in this section, "beneficiary" means the domestic insurer for whose benefit the letter of credit has been established and any successor of the beneficiary by operation of law. If a court of law appoints a successor in interest to the named beneficiary, then the named beneficiary includes and is limited to the court appointed domiciliary receiver (including conservator, rehabilitator or liquidator).

Drafting Note: The NAIC has adopted the above definition as part of the "Uniform Letter of Credit." However, the state may choose to utilize the following definition: "Beneficiary" includes any successor by operation of law of the named beneficiary, including without limitation any liquidator, rehabilitator, receiver or conservator.

B. The heading of the letter of credit may include a boxed section containing the name of the applicant and other appropriate notations to provide a reference for the letter of credit. The boxed section shall be clearly marked to indicate that such information is for internal identification purposes only.

C. The letter of credit shall contain a statement to the effect that the obligation of the qualified United States financial institution under the letter of credit is in no way contingent upon reimbursement with respect thereto.

D. The term of the letter of credit shall be for at least one year and shall contain an "evergreen clause" that prevents the expiration of the letter of credit without due notice from the issuer. The "evergreen clause" shall provide for a period of no less than thirty (30) days notice prior to expiration date or nonrenewal.

E. The letter of credit shall state whether it is subject to and governed by the laws of this state or the Uniform Customs and Practice for Documentary Credits of the International Chamber of Commerce Publication 600 (UCP 600) or International Standby Practices of the International Chamber of Commerce Publication 590 (ISP98), or any successor publication, and all drafts drawn thereunder shall be presentable at an office in the United States of a qualified United States financial institution.

F. If the letter of credit is made subject to the Uniform Customs and Practice for Documentary Credits of the International Chamber of Commerce Publication 600 (UCP 600) or International Standby Practices of the International Chamber of Commerce Publication 590 (ISP98), or any successor publication, then the letter of credit shall specifically address and provide for an extension of time to draw against the letter of credit in the event that one or more of the occurrences specified in Article 36 of Publication 600 or any other successor publication, occur.

G. If the letter of credit is issued by a financial institution authorized to issue letters of credit, other than a qualified United States financial institution as described in Subsection A of this section, then the following additional requirements shall be met:

   1. The issuing financial institution shall formally designate the confirming qualified United States financial institution as its agent for the receipt and payment of the drafts; and
   2. The "evergreen clause" shall provide for thirty (30) days notice prior to expiration date for nonrenewal.

H. Reinsurance agreement provisions.

   1. The reinsurance agreement in conjunction with which the letter of credit is obtained may contain provisions that:

(a) Require the assuming insurer to provide letters of credit to the ceding insurer and specify what they are to cover;

(b) Stipulate that the assuming insurer and ceding insurer agree that the letter of credit provided by the assuming insurer pursuant to the provisions of the reinsurance agreement may be drawn upon at any time, notwithstanding any other provisions in the agreement, and shall be utilized by the ceding insurer or its successors in interest only for one or more of the following reasons:

i. To pay or reimburse the ceding insurer for:

(I) The assuming insurer's share under the specific reinsurance agreement of premiums returned, but not yet recovered from the assuming insurers, to the owners of policies reinsured under the reinsurance agreement on account of cancellations of such policies;

(II) The assuming insurer's share, under the specific reinsurance agreement, of surrenders and benefits or losses paid by the ceding insurer, but not yet recovered from the assuming insurers, under the terms and provisions of the policies reinsured under the reinsurance agreement; and

(III) Any other amounts necessary to secure the credit or reduction from liability for reinsurance taken by the ceding insurer;

ii. Where the letter of credit will expire without renewal or be reduced or replaced by a letter of credit for a reduced amount and where the assuming insurer's entire obligations under the reinsurance agreement remain unliquidated and undischarged ten (10) days prior to the termination date, to withdraw amounts equal to the assuming insurer's share of the liabilities, to the extent that the liabilities have not yet been funded by the assuming insurer and exceed the amount of any reduced or replacement letter of credit, and deposit those amounts in a separate account in the name of the ceding insurer in a qualified U.S. financial institution apart from its general assets, in trust for such uses and purposes specified in Subsection H(1)(b)(i) of this section as may remain after withdrawal and for any period after the termination date.

(c) All of the provisions of Paragraph (1) of this subsection shall be applied without diminution because of insolvency on the part of the ceding insurer or assuming insurer.

2. Nothing contained Paragraph (1) of this subsection shall preclude the ceding insurer and assuming insurer from providing for:

(a) An interest payment, at a rate not in excess of the prime rate of interest, on the amounts held pursuant to Subparagraph (1)(b) of this subsection; or
(b) The return of any amounts drawn down on the letters of credit in excess of the actual amounts required for the above or any amounts that are subsequently determined not to be due.

Courtesy of Leah Campbell and Donald B. Henderson Jr., Wilkie Farr & Gallagher LLP

ASPATORE